Robert Frank's *The Americans*
The Art of Documentary Photography

Robert Frank's *The Americans*
The Art of Documentary Photography

Jonathan Day

intellect Bristol, UK / Chicago, USA

First published in the UK in 2011 by Intellect,
The Mill, Parnall Road, Fishponds, Bristol, BS16 3JG, UK

First published in the USA in 2011 by Intellect, The University of Chicago Press,
1427 E. 60th Street, Chicago, IL 60637, USA

A catalogue record for this book is available from the British Library.

Cover design: Holly Rose
Copy-editor: Sue Jarvis
Typesetting: John Teehan

ISBN 978-1-84150-315-8

Printed and bound by Gutenberg Press, Malta.

Contents

ACKNOWLEDGEMENTS

I would like to thank my children, Niimi and Miika Day-Gough, without whom none of this would have been worthwhile. My parents and sister, Janice and Peter Day and Susan Smith, have been unreservedly supportive through the years.

My friends Claire Gough, Nathan Tromans, Fergus Reid, Jared Jackson, Adam Beresford Brown and Edda Gerusel have seen me through many difficult moments on this journey. Simon Smith, Angela Vicari and Thom Livemore were wonderfully helpful during my time researching in Los Angeles and San Francisco. Thanks, Angela, for all those Valley Girl insights. Thanks also to the staff of the Los Angeles public library archives. Kristi Link Fernholz, Brad Fernholz, Jennifer Todd and Tony Derrick were wonderfully supportive during my research in the Mid-West. My mentors Kenneth Quickenden and George Noszlopy will see something of their approaches demonstrated in this book. My colleagues Chris O'Neil, David Durling, Mario Minichiello, Darren Newbury, Yvette Burn, Peter Windows, Julia Burdett and Yanyan Wang have been crucial to this effort and they have my sincere thanks.

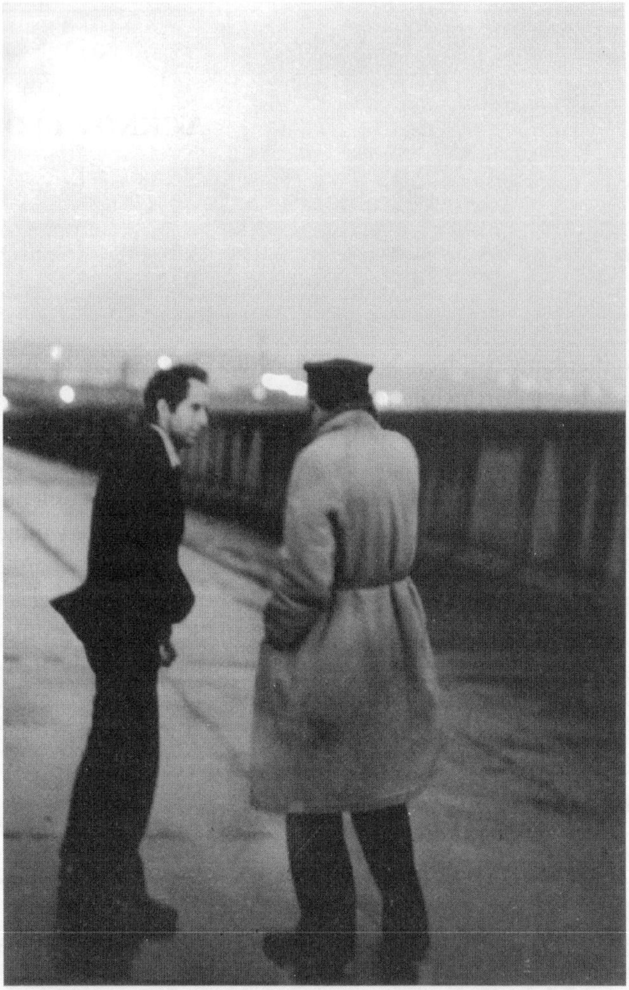

Robert Frank and musician Larry Rivers on a windswept causeway, New York, 1959. (Photo by John Cohen/Getty Images)

Foreword: Robert Frank

by Eamonn McCabe

I first met Robert Frank when he was in London for the opening of his show at Tate Modern in 2004. He didn't say much as I nervously tried to take a couple of photographs of the great man with my own Leica. We were both crammed in a tiny lift as we made our way up to his huge exhibition.

But Robert Frank never did say very much and there is not a single word by him in *The Americans*, his seminal book of photographs taken in just two years in the mid 1950s on a Guggenheim grant.

You get the impression that even the meagre captions at the end of the book were reluctantly dragged out of him by some poor curator or editor in search of at least some information about a set of some of the greatest photographs ever taken.

Jonathan Day in this book has expertly taken over as Frank's narrator, bravely describing each photograph and putting it into context with the other 82 in *The Americans*.

You should read this book and look at Frank's photographs while listening to some John Coltrane saxophone, preferably on an old record player crackling away in the background.

There are no rules in jazz and Frank broke all the rules with his Leica. There are heads missing in his pictures, but it makes them stronger. The face nearest you is often out of focus, but it makes the background even more powerful. His subjects rarely look at the camera, but you are engaged, you can't look away. The American flag is everywhere and threads through the whole book, binding it together.

As Jack Kerouac says in his introduction to *The Americans*

> "To Robert Frank I now give this message: You got eyes."

And now we have the words.

Eamonn McCabe was Picture Editor of The Guardian *from 1988 to 2001.*

FOREWORD: ROBERT FRANK

Introduction

This is an opinionated book. What strikes me first, every time I open Robert Frank's *The Americans*, is the strength and quality of its opinions. The photographs are the truth as Frank saw it. They are as honest, as poetic and as prophetic as Jack Kerouac's prose, Allen Ginsberg's poetry, Willem de Kooning's painting or John Coltrane's tenor saxophone playing. Frank knew the wonderful work of Walker Evans and so many others who had photographed America before him. And yet he had the temerity to believe he could do something different enough to matter, to be interesting and valuable. I am following his lead with this book, hoping that I too may have something interesting to say, in a way that does not exactly repeat what has gone before.

Frank wanted to see around and through the rhetoric of the American Dream, see beyond the idealism and gentility that blinkered and blinded Edward Steichen's *The Family of Man* exhibition and hamstrung so much of the photography that surrounded him. Frank wished, also, to avoid the commercial imperatives that had fuelled his earlier work in New York and which loomed over so much of the recording of America on film. The celebrated Standard Oil Picture File exemplifies this, interleaving documentary and dialectic, the propaganda of an oil company disguised as honest and sincere documents. Frank's no holds barred honesty is his book's strength. He was not seeking to praise or censure America; he simply sought to really see it. This is not surprising for a man who would be central to the 'Beat' group of artists, filming and recording them and their interests in Buddha's Dharma and Zen's emphasis on 'direct vision'. I don't apologize, then, for the opinionated nature of what you are about to read: Frank was looking to see America, and I too am looking to see Frank and his book.

I'm fascinated by these photographs and what they reveal about the society in which Frank lived and worked. The book was published in the year I was born: it helps explain my world. I have chosen to emphasize those materials that were near-contemporary with Frank's work: books, music, photographs and paintings shine a searchlight back on to this world that is lost to us now, staring mutely out of his pages. These 'texts' play a leading role here: expect to meet them more on this journey than works which belong to our world and our time. Nonetheless, anyone who ignores the wisdom of others is a fool, so this book uses and acknowledges the ideas of other lookers and thinkers without being a literature review. I wish to add to the literature around Frank, not to précis and summarize what has gone before.

The Americans is a complicated book. The photographs are often part of interconnected sequences—examining the nature of human love, for example, or the imagery of the cross. At the same time, many of them contribute to non-consecutive thematic considerations—the car, for instance, or the Stars and Stripes. These parallel devices work architecturally, knitting the book together like the interwoven trunks of a yew tree, or the convoluted fibres in jade. Extracting and describing these threads is a difficult business, and this book will approach and examine Frank's images in three ways.

First, the photographs are exploited as illustrations and indicators of the particular moment in time and space when Frank took his camera and made his record. *The Americans* is widely regarded as a milestone in the development of photography, and is also lauded as a ground-breaking exploration and examination of the emerging civilization of America. Despite all of this, when I flew to the States to see the excellent *Looking In* exhibition at the Museum of Modern Art in San Francisco, I was intrigued that this major retrospective was not advertised on the museum's plentiful hoardings, either outside the gallery or around the city. In alarm, I contacted the ticket office, which confirmed that the show was on and was available at no extra charge. An Ansel Adams and Georgia O'Keefe show was running upstairs from Frank's at the same gallery. Advertisements for this were plastered everywhere across the city; it carried an additional cover charge and was packed out. Frank's importance is acknowledged, but his book is, I suspect, not widely understood. In order to better understand the justifications for its accolades, we need to establish and examine the conditions under which *The Americans* was created. This will then allow us to approach the photographs appropriately. Only by unpicking the accretions of history that cling to Frank's images can we hope to see them 'directly' for themselves.

Second, the photographs are examined as aspects of the thematically driven discussion of America which Frank engaged in. The communicative power of Frank's work resides appreciably in the sophisticated construction of his argument. His critique of the American condition, and by extension the human condition, depends on these themed examinations, with which he stitches his book together. Many readers and writers have found *The Americans* baffling, flabbergasted by its densely packed and multi-layered imagery. Examining the thematic threads facilitates an entry into the depths of the book, offering us a key, a kind of Rosetta stone if you will. Themes sometimes exist around a particular repeated visual strophe, the car, for example, or the flag. Other considerations are more notional, the imaging of new American 'icons', appropriate to a developing romance with materialism and consumerism, is an instance. These themes are balanced by others that develop out of Frank's reactive image-making. His debunking of *The Family of Man* exhibition is an example, as is his recontextualizing of elements seen in advertising imagery.

Third and finally, the photographs are examined as constituent moments in an extended photographic sequence. Alongside all of their cultural and photographic-historical significance, and notwithstanding their contribution to the book's complex thematic constructions, it is useful to examine the photographs simply as a series of pictures. This is no simple task, given Frank's dislike of the linear narrative. Nonetheless, many images display linking motifs or notions. Sometimes these commonalities exist as considerations spread across a number of photographs; sometimes they can be found in the repetition of the smallest of visual sigils. Often, and impressively, photographs are linked both backwards into a set that is finishing and forwards into what is to follow. There are diptychs, triptychs and quadtychs here, and even sometimes pairs of triptychs, which echo each other across the pages. *The Americans* is in many ways structured like music, with repetitions, recapitulations and even notable *caesuras*—moments when everything is brought to a stop, facilitating consideration and recuperation.

Each of us naturally and rightly approaches writing in our own way. If we accord Frank the privilege of dismissing notions of linear structure, and even admire him for it, why should we as readers have to approach this or any other book in that way? I have designed this book as a thing that can be comfortably read from start to finish. If a reader prefers, however, each of the three sections is sufficiently self-contained to be read independently. If your interest is in the details of the photographs, for example, then you may wish to go directly to Part Two or Three, perhaps returning later to examine the context in which the works were produced. None of the writing is repeated across sections. When the same image is considered several times, there will inevitably be some overlap, but one of the joys of Frank's multi-faceted complexity is the obviation of the need for repetition. His three years of work, and the lifetime before in which Frank was journeying towards this place, requires, rather, complementary considerations of the same photographs.

From early on in the planning of this book, my lovely editor and I decided that trying to reproduce Frank's images here would be rather pointless. The excellent recent Steidl reprint[1] is very attractively priced and will illustrate the considerations presented here much better than a few piecemeal illustrations might.[2] I have referred to Frank's images by their captions, declining to use any numerical reference since none exists in the book itself. Since all the images in the book were made in 1955 and 1956 and are held now by the National Gallery, Washington DC, I will avoid constant and tedious repetition of this information in attributions.

In order to best appreciate the moment being celebrated by both Frank and this book, I would recommend the following: Jack Kerouac's novel *On the Road* (written 1955–

56), Alan Ginsberg's *Howl* (1956), the paintings of Jackson Pollock, Willem de Kooning and Jasper Johns, and the music of Woody Guthrie, Charlie Parker and John Coltrane. Equally useful, though rather more arcane, is a good collection of Zen works—perhaps *Writings from the Zen Masters* (Various 2009).

There are a number of texts that will support our investigation, and I recommend them wholeheartedly. *Looking In* (Greenough 2009) is an excellent resource, providing an encyclopaedic range of facsimiles and images, principally from the collection of the National Gallery, Washington DC, accompanied by extensive annotations. Anne Tucker and Phillip Brookman's *Robert Frank: New York to Nova Scotia* (1986) and the video that accompanied it are also very interesting. Walker Evans' *American Photographs* is the nearest thing to a template for *The Americans* and is well worth looking at. The catalogue to *The Family of Man* exhibition (1955) is one of the most popular books of photographs ever produced and is easily available in a number of imprints. The newer ones have beautiful reproductions, but the originals have that special something which only time and age can bring. Ulrich Keller produced his fascinating *The Highway as Habitat: A Roy Stryker Documentation, 1943–1955* in 1986, which is a great source book for photographs and information on Standard Oil's Picture File. Finally *The Pictures are a Necessity: Robert Frank in Rochester, NY November 1988* is a wonderful collection, particularly because of the unusually revealing conversations and letters between Robert Frank and William S. Johnson. It seems strangely appropriate that this latter is very hard to find.

Notes

1. Steidl have this to say about their reprint:

   > In July 2007 the Steidl edition of *The Americans* was printed. Frank was involved in every step of its design and production. The 83 photographs were scanned in tritone at Steidl's digital darkroom from vintage prints in Frank's collection … (http://www.steidlville.com/books/695-The-Americans.html, accessed 17 January 2010).

2. The images included are, instead, mostly of Frank, his friends and his associates.

Part One

America and *The Americans*

There are a variety of approaches to history. This may seem a strange way to begin our account, but it is of foundational importance. The outrageous, if possibly short lived, success of our species has developed out of survival imperatives which cause us to observe, analyze, predict and control our environment and the other beings with whom we share our world. We are, then, creatures who look obsessively for patterns. Think of our bizarre but wonderful ability to decode random-looking mathematically generated dots in so-called *Magic Eye* pictures. We look and look until the Statue of Liberty or some other such is revealed. After the epiphany, after the pattern has been resolved and meaning has been recognized, we are satisfied and never need to look there again. This desire for pattern and meaning is also inescapably present in the assessment and telling of history. There is comfort in a hermetic, tidy account of the past, and comfort too in a measured and recognizable voice, leading us through those long ago and lost intricacies. I am delighted and honoured that you have chosen to vouchsafe me some moments of your time and I hope that my voice will not grate and strain through these few pages, but I also hope that it is not all that you will hear. I have tried whenever possible to let the original and authentic voices speak, the people who were there, living, vital, passionate and involved. I want to try to hear their footsteps and see their expressions as when, for example, Louis Faurer walked for the first time into the studios of *Harper's Junior Bazaar* at Madison and 56th and met Robert Frank. I want to smell the city air on the evening sidewalk as Frank asked Kerouac to write his introduction.

I am not claiming to be absent in this account—it is unavoidably me linking these moments together and navigating a course—but I want the picture I paint of this past to be collaged out of the scraps we have left, the moments and memories of the people I quote and thus invoke. It is my hope that the materials I present will validate the account and that these original voices will be the sound in your ears as you read, the sound of history, garbled and crackling like an old valve radio, the sound of the people who made us, the sound of the past.

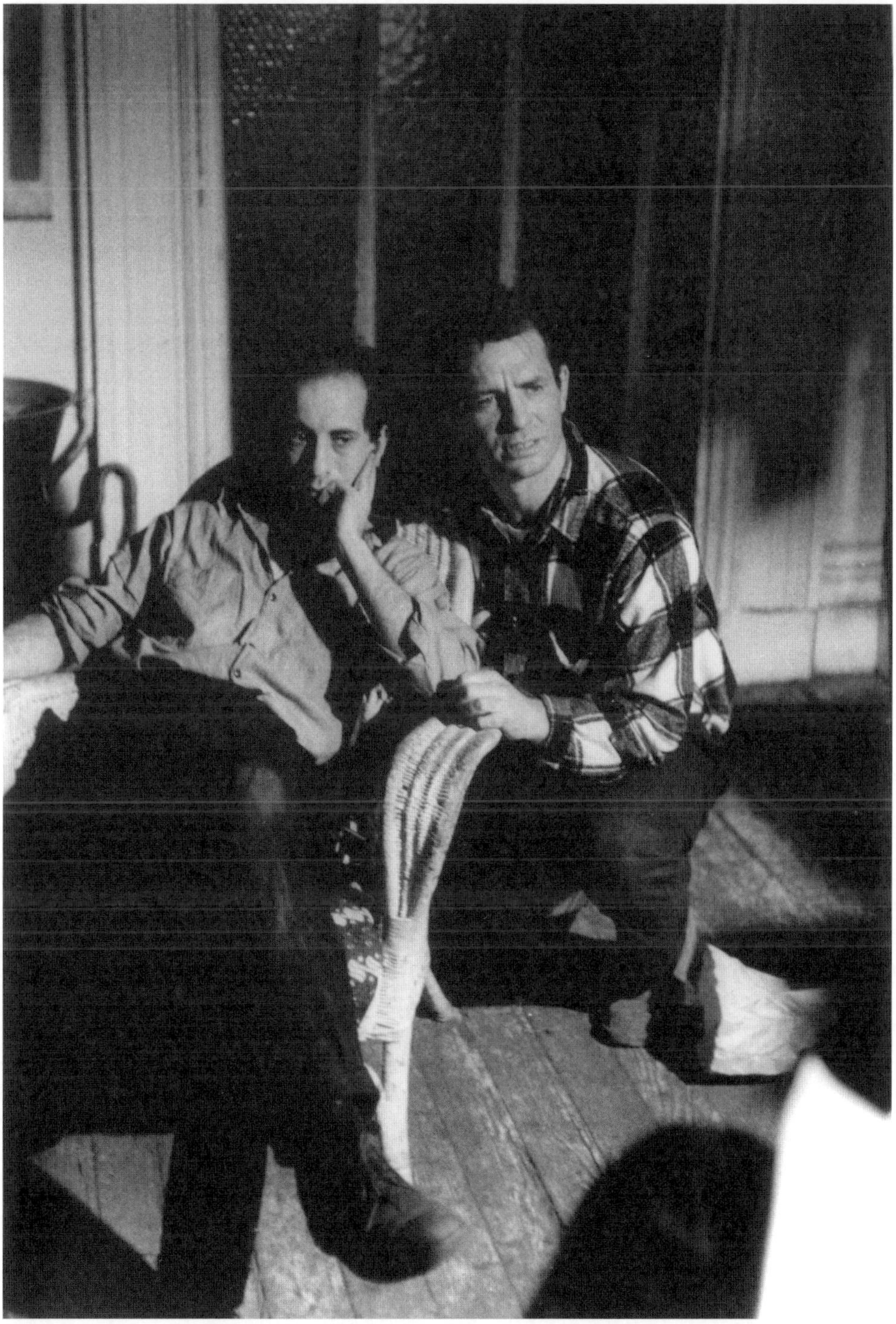

Robert Frank and Jack Kerouac almost exactly a year before the Americans was released in the US. Greenwich Village, New York, 1959. (Photo by John Cohen/Getty Images)

1

FRANK AND THE '50S

> What a poem this is, what poems can be written about this book of pictures some day by some young new writer high by candlelight bending over them describing every gray mysterious detail, the gray film that caught the actual pink juice of human kind… (Kerouac in Frank 1959: 3)

> These souvenirs of the past…are partly hidden and curiously resonant, bringing messages which may or may not be welcome, may or may not be real. Disturbing ideas which have a tale to tell or just lie mutely, often justifying the interest one might take in them. (Frank 1991: before plate 1)

> …lying in wait, pursuing, sometimes catching the essence of the black and white, the knowledge of where God is. (Frank 1991: after plate 63)

Can you imagine it? Afternoon turning to evening in a canyon-like New York street, long shadows falling across a young man sitting in the driver's seat of a Ford Business Coupe. The back seat is strewn with his gear and his children, and a Leica shares the front seat with his wife. The enormous expanse of wild America is out there, opened up by highways and interstates, a largely unknown, obscure and guessed-at land, waiting for his wheels and shutter. All around him writers scrawl, making novels in three weeks, saxophonists and trumpeters wail, and poets howl. All of them are desperate to capture this new, never-before-experienced moment, change so palpably in the air, before the arguments are settled and the moment lost. We are sitting here now, 50ish years later, holding in our hands the souvenir he left us of his journey. Long considered and prepared with immense care, it is a mostly wordless, wonderfully eloquent book, describing the world he encountered, his images shaped and selected according to the dictates of his understanding and imagination. It's a world lost to us now, but near enough in memory to tug at the strings of our recollections and to massage the intuitions of our own histories. I was born in the year *The Americans* was published: its story is also my story.

How do we describe Robert Frank? How can the conditions that climaxed in *The Americans* be understood? What in his makeup, his history and experience led him to drive out across that enormous country, exactly as Jack Kerouac was rendering everything associated with the American road iconic for a generation?

Robert Frank was born in 1924 in Switzerland and grew up as a wealthy Jewish child in Zurich. His father was a businessman and Frank was expected to follow in his footsteps:

> I didn't know exactly what I wanted to be but I knew what I didn't want. Switzerland was a very traditional place where you were expected to do what your father did—follow some sort of directions that were laid down. I didn't want the restrictions of life that my parents had, their concerns about money and respectability and all. I took up photography as a first little step to get out of the orbit that they prescribed for me. (Frank in Johnson 1989: 28)

He chose to decline his expected role in his father's business, and studied photography instead. He worked hard and was acknowledged and liked in the Swiss photographic community.

The turmoil and tragedy of the Second World War had an unavoidable influence on Frank:

> The war was interesting—the fear that I saw in my parents. If Hitler invaded Switzerland—and there was very little to stop him—that would have been the end of them. It was an unforgettable situation. I watched the grown ups decide what to do—when to change your name, whatever. It's on the radio everyday. You hear that guy [Hitler] talking—threatening—cursing the Jews. It's forever in your mind—like a smell, the voice of that man—of Goering, of Goebbels—these were evil characters. Of course you're impressed… Being Jewish and living with the threat of Hitler must have been a very big part of my understanding… (Frank in Johnson 1989: 26–27)

Instead of settling into his Swiss Jewish photographic world, he again defeated expectations and moved to Paris, and then New York:

> The war was over and I wanted to get out of Switzerland. I didn't want to build my future there. The country was too closed, too small for me. When I got to America I saw right away that everything was open, that you could do anything. And how you were accepted depended on what you did with it. You could work to satisfy what was in you. Once I came to America I knew I wouldn't go back. (Frank in Johnson 1989: 28–29)

He was a runaway, a young adventurous photographer driven, along with so many others, by the squall of disbelief and revulsion generated by the destruction and genocide of the Second World War, to the unknown and exciting shores of America. A middle-class European kid who was confronted suddenly by all that the Jazz Age and the nascent Beatnik culture had to offer. New York, when he arrived, had a culture peopled by émigré artists like Piet Mondrian, Willem de Kooning and Mark Rothko, who had moved there as a result of the war. They lived alongside exciting homegrown talents like Jackson Pollock and Barnett Newman. Wonderfully, though, it wasn't just painting that was happening. Here was the opportunity to listen to Charlie Parker, John Coltrane and the thousand other Bop players in cellars and clubs. Woody Guthrie, the darling of well-heeled, middle-class American radicals desperate for some working-class authenticity, was telling everyone, 'This land is your land.' Hipster writers like Jack Kerouac and Allen Ginsberg were experimenting and subverting literary expectations, experiments so radical that a ban of Ginsberg's book *Howl* (1956) was attempted, only to be defeated by the San Francisco bookstore that published it. The rigid social demarcations of Europe were blurred and muddied in this New World.

Something certainly needed to change. How long could humanity continue its cycles of uneasy peace and all-out war? How many had to die before someone solved the Old World riddle? Where were the saviours? Twice in 30 years Europe had hovered at the brink of annihilation. After the First World War, the Dadaist, Surrealist and *Neue Sacklichkeit* artists had sung, painted and performed their objections. The League of Nations was formed so that such a catastrophe could never happen again. There's an irony. The writer Albert Camus and others saw the Absurd as the only description and explanation for the insoluble agony and contradictions of human existence. Sisyphus, who in legend repeatedly pushed his rock to the top of the mountain only to see it plunge down again as a punishment for denying the Gods, was crowned Camus' hero (Camus 1942). Since life is absurd and there is no recourse to the hope or relief of any other world, Camus argued, this doomed man, accepting his lot and smiling defiance into the teeth of fate, was the ideal model for us all. This 'taking it on the chin' stance is important. The period during which Frank conceived and executed his project was the time of the 'Birth of the Cool' in jazz music. Leroi Jones described this stance:

> The term *cool* in its original context meant a specific reaction to the world, a specific relationship to one's environment. To be cool was, in its most accessible meaning, to be calm, even unimpressed, by what horror the world might daily propose. (Jones 1963, in Wall 2009)

Trumpeter Miles Davis was the midwife at the Birth of the Cool. He knew the writer and philosopher John Paul Sartre, a contemporary of Camus, thanks to his *Parisienne* girlfriend and muse, Juliet Greco. Miles famously said 'for me, music and life are all about style' (Wall 2009).

Camus' ideas filled the playhouses in works by Ionesco, Genet and others. These trickled out into cinema, as *Rebel Without a Cause* (Ray 1955) and *The Wild One* (Benedek 1954) heralded emergent youth culture and elevated the energy of working people. Films like *A Streetcar Named Desire* (Kazan 1951) revealed ghetto romances to be as profound as those imaged in any Old World 'high' culture, just as *The Grapes of Wrath* (Ford 1940) had revealed the true heroism of the world in the form of a broken-hearted mother saving a dying man with the literal milk of human kindness.

European culture was redundant. All its finery and refinement had only led to the palace and the workhouse, to the battlefield and to death. Wilfred Owen spoke for so many young Europeans when he wrote in 1918: 'I would have poured my spirit without stint. But not through wounds; not on the cess of war.' (Owen 1994: 60) The only thing the proud and potent movers and shakers of the Old World truly owned was shame.

Something new was badly needed, and clearly it was likely to come from somewhere other than Europe. If Old World leaders were revealed as compromised, acquisitive and self-seeking, then the people destined to save the world would come from somewhere other than the ruling class. In the 1958 *US Camera* annual, edited by Tom Maloney, Walker Evans wrote an introduction to a series of Frank's Guggenheim-funded photographs. He underlined this search, quoting George Santayana:

> In the classical and romantic tradition of Europe, love, of which there was very little, was supposed to be kindled by beauty, of which there was a great deal; perhaps moral chemistry may be able to reverse this operation, and in the future and in America it may breed beauty out of love. (Maloney 1958: 90)

America had a tradition of levelling classes. It was not a commonwealth by any means, but notions of birth were, and are, less significant than wealth. This social and philosophical position led, as much as anything, to the 'American System of Manufactures' (Mayr and Post 1981). This was the revolution in industrial production that so signally undermined European practices of class-appropriate consumption and, surreptitiously, therefore the class system. The method, pioneered in Smith's Armoury in Connecticut, and then in factories run by Singer, Colt and Ford, insisted on the interchangeability of parts. This standardization allowed items to be repaired easily. The mechanization needed to achieve interchangeability led to the production line, the division of labour and ultimately to mass production. Every item from a production line was designed to be near identical. This didn't result in higher quality or more intrinsic beauty in objects *per se*, but it meant that functional objects could be produced much more cheaply and in greater quantities. Crucially, it meant that identical products were available to everyone, regardless of status. In Frank's time, the 'American System' had already contributed significantly to the winning of the second World War by the Allies, and mass-produced 'consumer goods' would radically reshape the world. This revolution was coming out of America.

In response to European decadence and failure, artists as well as writers looked to the common man and woman, and the rhythms of everyday ordinariness, for salvation. Gone and going were the love of the artist hero, standing high on some metaphorical cliff, at whose work and life the rest of us could only look with wonder, as she or he lived life with an intensity unavailable to the common person (see the celebrated Casper David Friedrich painting *Wanderer Above the Sea of Fog*, 1818, Kunsthalle, Hamburg). The tawdry and commonplace was the new place to be. Thus the passion of the music of the fields and factories (Guthrie) was played alongside the strange and wonderful syntheses of the ghettos, where Black, Jewish and Irish modalities spewed out 'jazz'. This twisting and mercurial music never stood still long enough to be properly grasped, understood or categorized. The rhythms and vocabulary of the 'hip' street speech of poor people were incarnated in the works of the 'Beat poets' (Cuirara 2002). All of this life, dismissed so often as 'low' or vernacular culture, seemed for the first time to hold within it, secreted away and kept from the view of the intelligentsia and elite, the secret ciphers of salvation. The 'art' of the everyday—hand-painted billboards, street furniture and vernacular architecture—were the subjects of serious photography (Walker Evans and the Farm Security Administration are examples), which was no longer reserved for reactions to the sublime vastness of Yosemite (Ansell Adams) or the isolated sensuality of natural forms (Edward Weston). Not surprisingly, workers became the new heroes. Dorothea Lange made her *Migrant Mother* photograph as potent as any previous depiction of the Madonna and Child, picturing the suffering woman who must bear all pain for the sake of her children and yet survive (1936, F S A archive, Library of Congress). Another of her photographs, depicting a woman standing in ploughed fields, testifies silently to the challenges of existence with which she is still so palpably grappling. Her *White Angel* (1934, National Gallery of Canada) speaks eloquently of white-knuckle survival in the face of adversity, which was all too familiar still in the 1950s. Don't confuse these works, though, with Socialist works made in Russia and China. There the workers pictured were generic 'everymen', stripped of specificity and individuality. These American heroes were real individuals, with complex characters and histories on display.

The picturing of this world was not always positive or sympathetic. These were not all eulogies. Many observers questioned and tested these ideas. Walker Evans exhibits a notable emotional distance in much of his work. He presents his working men, women and children for scrutiny, without the embodied empathy of Lange's photographs. In his search for beauty and meaning, he imaged bare-board interiors and the poor families who lived therein. Nonetheless, his precise and analytic pictures record his quest for the stigmata of this working-class salvation, one that he insists must be demonstrable, robust and resolute. As James Agee, with whom Evans collaborated on their book *Let Us Now Praise Famous Men* wrote:

> this square home as it stands in unshadowed earth between the winding years of heaven, is, not to me but of itself, one among the serene and final uncapturable beauties of existence. (Agee and Evans 1941: 24)

His emotional distance from his subjects did not prevent him looking for beauty within their creations, even if he did sometimes feel it necessary to 'assist' them with their designs.

This drift towards the working class was leading some artists to question their concerns. While many, certainly, continued in the Modernist tradition, other artists were reacting against these perennial themes with boredom and irritation. Jackson Pollock, in the tradition of the tortured artist-hero, explored the potentials of the relationship between his body, paint and canvas in his 'gestural' or 'action' paintings, controlling the fall of pigment with the finely controlled motor skills of a surgeon or pianist. Mark Rothko followed the mystical route, travelling further into the relationship between colour, form and the transcendent than anyone before him. Willem de Kooning continued Picasso's exploration of the darker side of male understanding and imagining of women. Jasper Johns, seemingly bored with all this, made his enormously eloquent American flag from melted wax (*Flag*, 1954, Museum of Modern Art, New York), while Ray Johnson held up Elvis (*Elvis Presley No. 2*, 1956, collection of William S. Wilson), a singer who had grown up with poor blacks, as the new icon, the new hero. Robert Rauschenberg ironically commented on the global dissemination of consumer culture in his *Coca-Cola Plan* (1958, Museum of Contemporary Art, Los Angeles), situating empty Coke bottles between renaissance *putti* wings. He also bought and erased a de Kooning sketch, which he then exhibited, just in case anyone had missed the point (*Erased de Kooning Drawing*, 1953, San Francisco Museum of Modern Art). Politics and specific social concerns were being figured literally in the visual arts, eschewing the more established allegorical approaches. Change and revolution were in the air, in the arts as much as in politics.

From regimented, polite and genteel Switzerland, Robert Frank stepped on to the streets of this wild, anarchic and exciting world as a stranger from another land, an outsider. This has always been an advantage for poets and prophets: 'no prophet is accepted in his own country' (Luke the Evangelist n.d.: chapter 4: 24).

2

Developing *The Americans*

Frank's photography before *The Americans*

When he arrived in New York in 1947, Frank brought *40 Fotos,* a book maquette he had made in Switzerland, with him. His photographic apprenticeship had been thorough and he had worked hard, evidenced in this hand bound collection of finely detailed studio compositions and studies of people at parades and festivals, created during 1945 and 1946. John Szarkowski, curator of photography at the Museum of Modern Art from 1963, remembers:

> Robert's earlier work…was very much of a piece with the kind of photography that was coming out of Europe after the war. It was much more romantic, moodier…it was not difficult to take. It was in its essence…conventional. (Livingston 1992: 308)

Much of Frank's work resembled that of many of his famous European predecessors. The geometry of Moholy-Nagy is reflected in his *Rue de la Santé* (1950, collection of June Leaf) or his *34th Street, New York* (1949, collection of Robert Delpire). The social documentary of Bill Brandt's *The English at Home* (1936) informs Frank's *Paris, Porte de Clignancourt, 1949* (collection of Robert Delpire) or his *Caereu, Wales, 1951* (collection of Robert Delpire). He echoes Henri Cartier-Bresson's joviality in his *Fairground, Paris, 1950* (collection of June Leaf) and even recalls Eugene Atget in *Flower Barrow, Paris, 1949* (collection of June Leaf). Being compared to such luminaries is powerful praise, but Frank wanted more—he was ambitious and restless. He saw that America was the place for him to develop:

> America was a good climate to do something that wasn't possible for me in Switzerland. I didn't want to be an 'artist' but I wanted to be respected for what I would put out. Photography wasn't an 'art' then, but I knew that you could somehow make pictures that were different from 99 percent of what you saw. I didn't think of that as art; I felt it was just my way of expressing something. (Frank, in Johnson 1989: 29)

Frank showed his *40 Fotos* to Alexey Brodovitch, who hired him as a photographer for *Harper's Bazaar*. He recalls, 'I got to know Brodovitch quite well and he really knew photography. His book on the ballet influenced me.' (Frank, in Johnson 1989: 29) Frank was now a photojournalist by profession, and it would seem he was reasonably happy thus. Louis Faurer remembers:

> It was in the fall of 1947 that I first met Robert. The person who introduced us was Lillian Bassman, she was assisting Alexey Brodovitch. When I walked in there, into the working area, the studio they called it, there was one person—and it was Robert. We began to communicate immediately. He told me that he had lived in Zurich and had just been in New York a bit over six months. We both laughed at a lot of things, at what was going on around us in that place. Robert used to say, 'what a town, what a town, it could only happen here, it couldn't happen in any other town.' (Livingston 1992: 308)

This apparent acceptance and enjoyment of his new home and new role are evident in Frank's undertakings and in his work. He said:

> It would have been terrible for me to have stayed in Europe… I learned everything from being around good people. It was a very good time. It (New York) wasn't as crowded as it is today… My affair with new York—that city; that's my interaction with New York and I feel I have a certain gratitude… They have made me what I am and they have given me a lot. (Frank, in Johnson 1989: 32–33)

Frank became part of this world.

A close association developed between Frank and the very established photographer and curator Edward Steichen. Steichen was a 'grand old man' of photography by this time, having been central to the celebrated 'Photo-Secession' group in New York, a group that trumpeted and lobbied for the recognition of photography as art. Its very name was borrowed from the various European avant-garde groups that had used that description for themselves. By the time Frank met him, Steichen had become curator of photography at the Museum of Modern Art in New York. Their friendship resulted in Frank's inclusion, amusingly, in both the *51 American Photographers* exhibition in 1950 and in the *Post-War European Photography* show in 1953 (both Museum of Modern Art, New York), highlighting his rather mercurial position within this photographic *milieu*. Steichen and Frank travelled together while the older photographer was researching his celebrated *The Family of Man* exhibition (1955, Museum of Modern Art, New York). Frank was a face on the New York photographic scene. He was involved with photographers who would later be grouped together as the 'New York School'. The group's visual *esprit de corps* can be observed in Frank's work from that time. 'People You Don't See' was a series of images of New Yorkers that Frank took in August of 1951, and submitted to the annual Young Photographers' Contest at *Life* magazine. He included *On Saturday and Sunday the street is empty and Georgie is alone* (1951, National Gallery of Art, Washington) in this series. The photograph clearly echoes other studies of New York childhood by contemporary photographers, in particular Helen Levitt's *New York, 1945* (collection of Helen Levitt). Both photographs contrast the wide-eyed naiveté of children with the pragmatic world of the city street. There are intriguing moments in which several New York photographers capture and comment on the same scenes and moments, as one would expect a group of friends to do. Sidney Grossman's *San Gennaro Festival, Mulberry Street, New York City* (1948, collection M. Grossman-Cohen) features a myriad bulbs arching across the darkness of a New York night. In his *Medals/New York* (1951, National Gallery of Art, Washington), Frank juxtaposes the light caught in a vendor's medal chains with that of similar electric arches above. Louis Faurer's photograph of Frank and his wife at the San Gennaro festival in the same year reveals these as the same arches. Frank's *Central Park South* (1948, Pace-McGill Gallery, New York) of 1948 explores two of New York's most recognized icons, the Empire State Building and the nose of a cab, and comments on the nature of photography as it captures reflections of these in a puddle. Louis Faurer's *Staten Island Ferry, New York City* (1946, collection of D. Bell) records the city in a similar way, caught on the famous ferry's window. Both images glory in the flat, illusory immateriality of reflections, exploiting them as an analogue for photography.

As well as photographers, Frank associated with painters and filmmakers. Willem de Kooning lived across the yard from Frank and, as Philip Brookman says in a letter to Jane Livingston, shared Frank's belief that photography was an art form equal to painting (Livingston 1992: 360). Frank's intellectual involvement with the New York avant-garde was crucial to his work, his sense of self and his sense of mission.[1]

Frank had become a successful photojournalist. Walker Evans wrote of him:

> Two examples of Frank's superiority come to mind: A set of photographs he made in a Welsh mining town Caerau, a few years ago, picturing the life of one coal miner there. And currently, a journalistic commission he executed for me at Fortune, of the Pennsylvania Railroad's

> Congressional Limited train. Both these projects—one freely inspired, one commercial—are creative, thorough and intelligent. Which leads me to remark that, after all intelligence is a gift, too, which I should have claimed in the list for Frank. I may seem to abandon all restraint in praise here; this would be wrong; Frank has made his mistakes. He once tried to photograph one city block, and failed to sustain a level of quality, I thought. Yet in the Welsh miner series there was poetry. And in the Congressional Limited assignment he showed how resourceful a cameraman can and ought to be. (Evans 1955, in Greenough 2009: 152)

Despite his success and ability to earn a living, it was clear from early on that Frank had reservations. He said later of magazine work:

> …for me to be working on assignment for a magazine. It suggests to me the feeling of a hack writer or a commercial illustrator. Since I sense that my ideas, my mind and my eye are not creating the picture but that the editors' minds and eyes will finally determine which of my pictures will be reproduced to suit the magazine's purposes. I have a genuine distrust and *me*fiance toward all group activities. Mass production of uninspired photojournalism and photography without thought becomes anonymous merchandise. The air becomes infected with the smell of photography. (Frank, in Maloney 1958: 115)

This may seem damning, but others echoed Frank's sentiments. William Manchester described some press photographers thus:

> In the main they lack imagination, a sense of composition and an awareness of what Henri Cartier-Bresson called 'the decisive moment'. Most men lugging Sun Speed Graphics around didn't even know it existed. (Manchester 1989)

Frank complained about the disempowerment of photographers by the magazines for which they worked. Wilson Hicks, a picture editor at *Life* magazine, claimed that 'cameramen are too involved with their work to have sound judgement concerning its editorial packaging and publication' (Hicks 1952: 41ff., 128ff.). In his *The Highway as Habitat: A Roy Stryker Documentation,* Ulrich Keller usefully describes the editorial process:

> Rigid procedures at *Life* and *Look* denied most cameramen any input other than photographic raw materials. In the picture press, photographers were little wheels in a large machinery based on minute division of

> labour. More often than not the story idea originated from editorial staff; it was then developed by researchers and writers; only at a relatively late point the photographer got involved to shoot the fully plotted and approved story on location, usually under the supervision of the writer and under a tight deadline. The selection of pictures, their co-ordination with captions and text, the visual presentation and the ideological 'slant' of the story—all these matters lay in the hands of numerous specialists from lay-out man to art director. As a result the published picture essay often bore little resemblance to what the photographer had actually seen and felt and documented. (Keller 1986: 23)

Many magazines, then, almost discouraged vision on the part of the photographer. They were craftsmen who fulfilled a role, obeyed a brief.

Frank's unhappiness with his situation did not pass unnoticed. Lou Silverstein, a friend and colleague, commented:

> I don't think Robert was trying to knock the establishment…but I guess he was trying to keep himself free of the contaminating influences of commercial life. I have no doubt that while other guys were applying after-shave lotion, Robert was making sure that his lining was going to be just irritatingly enough out to let people know what was up. (Livingston 1992: 307)

Frank was searching for another way forward. He recalls that, while working for Alexey Brodovitch:

> Kertesz's book [*Day of Paris*] moved me and then I looked at his work in *House and Garden*. In the back of my mind I always thought about him. He taught me something about how if you have to you can make a living that way. One is commercial work and one is the other work. Kertesz was in my world [commercial photography] and he really did produce something good. Not like the big names of fashion photography who commanded tremendous attention and who were extremely well paid. And what did they do? His book and Brandt's work made me more ambitious to be like them—to produce work that would be good and not simply commercial. (Frank, in Johnson 1989: 29–30)

Frank sensed that something more was possible and wanted to explore it. It was time to move on:

> Brodovitch was interested in producing the magazine and he turned everything to that direction. He tried to make me into a fashion photographer. And as for the staff photographers at *Bazaar,* there was no spirit there. The only thing that mattered was to make more money. I knew that I could not gain by staying in that atmosphere very much longer … I realized that security didn't matter. I could never have the security that I had in Switzerland, so there was no reason for me to attempt to get into that high-fashion world. (Frank, in Johnson 1989: 30)

Frank decided to try another approach:

> I went to Peru to satisfy my own nature, to be free to work for myself… I was very free with the camera. I didn't think of what would be the correct thing to do; I did what I felt good doing. I was like an action painter. From 1947 to 1950 it was like I was in training camp, I tried things out. I learned about life. (Frank, in Johnson 1989: 30)

Most significantly, he compared himself with the 'action' or 'gestural' painters working at that time in New York, also known as the Abstract Expressionists. He was moving inexorably into an assessment of his photography as part of the nebulous and indeterminate notion of 'art'. This would become overt and self-avowed after the completion of the project that resulted in *The Americans*. In a statement printed alongside a collection of his images in the *US Camera* annual of 1958, he commented:

> If the photographer wants to be an artist, his thoughts cannot be developed overnight in the corner drugstore. I am not a pessimist, but looking at a contemporary picture magazine makes it difficult for me to speak about the advancement of photography, since photography is accepted today without questions and is also presumed to be understood by all—even children. I feel that only the integrity of the individual photographer can raise its level. (Frank, in Maloney 1958: 115)

By this time, vision had become essential to Frank. He sought 'the advancement of photography' through 'the integrity of the individual photographer'. He wanted to do more than simply document, acknowledging that photography is never objective, and thus running against the view still held by many who were involved in documentary work at the time. Frank felt:

> There is one thing the photograph must contain, the humanity of the moment. This kind of photography is realism. But realism is not

> enough—there has to be vision, and the two together can make a good photograph. It is difficult to describe this thin line where matter ends and mind begins. (Frank 1961: 22)

As part of his 'moving on', Frank focused on other outlets for his work. He exhibited at the Tibor de Nagy Gallery with Ben Schulz and W. Eugene Smith in 1951 and at Helen Gee's Limelight Coffeehouse (Bunnell 1977). He had work published in some European periodicals, including the September and December 1952 issues of *Neuf*. These magazines were perceived very differently from *Harper's Bazaar*. In the same year, some of Frank's work was included in the *Welt Austellung der Photographie* at the Lucerne Kunsthaus. However, it is not his interest in and success with gallery shows that defines his most famous photographic achievement, but his interest in the book.

The photographic book

The photographic book was becoming increasingly popular with many photographers at the time. One reason was the relative lack of exhibition opportunities. Illustrated exhibition catalogues were also uncommon. These factors left little choice for photographers who sought something more for their work than the transient disposability of *The New York Times* or *Life*. There were a number of significant models around for Frank to peruse. Margaret Bourke-White and Erskine Caldwell had produced their *You Have Seen Their Faces* in 1937, a book chronicling the lives of poor Southern people during the Depression. Robert Capa's book about the Spanish Civil War, *Death in the Making* (1938), and, far more importantly for Frank, Walker Evans' *American Photographs* were both published in 1938. Significant among the books that followed were Weegee's *Naked City* of 1945, a small-format (6 by 9 inches) book, apparently organized as a series of jokes, and Henri Cartier-Bresson's *The Decisive Moment* (1952), which was commercially successful in Europe and America.

Frank had been interested in the book as an outlet for work since his time in Switzerland. We have noted his creation of the handmade folio *40 Fotos*. He followed this with a book *maquette* of photographs taken in Peru, which he gave to his mother for her birthday, and a book he made for Mary Lockspeiser, who he would later marry. In 1951 he created *Black, White and Things* in collaboration with designer Werner Zyrd. In 1956, his friend Robert Delpire published *Indiens Pas Morts* in Paris; this was a book of photographs taken in Bolivia and Peru by Frank, with additional images by Walter Bischof and Pierre Verger. In 1957 the *New York Times* published *New York Is*, a collection of 24 of Frank's photographs created as a promotional book.

As Frank was preparing *The Americans*, William Klein's *New York: Life is Good and Good for You in New York* (1956) was published. Interestingly, this was first released in France, as *The Americans* would be. Photographer Richard Avedon, designer Alexei Brodovitch and writer Truman Capote were also working on their influential *Observations* (1959). The use of the book format by such influential artists reveals its principal attribute: along with the exhibition, it legitimized photography as something other than commercial work, something like 'art'. The unlikelihood of profit further underlined the lack of commerciality. Frank, for example, received a payment of $250 from Grove Press for *The Americans*.

The Guggenheim Fellowship

In order to continue his pursuit of a personal photography, perhaps photography for its own sake, isolated from corrupting and debasing commercial factors, Frank needed to find funds. After all, he had a young family to support. He decided to apply to the Guggenheim Foundation. Although many photographers had received awards, Frank would be the first European to do so. Grant funding would allow him to make his own decisions throughout the creation of his work.

The virtue of this path was not universally recognized. William Klein 'liked the idea of making a living with one hand and doing exactly what you wanted with the other. I felt this relationship was more comfortable than grant hustling.' (Klein, in Livingston 1992: 312) Frank had no such scruples. Guggenheim Fellowships were very well respected. In his introduction to some of Frank's Fellowship photographs, published in 1958 by *US Camera*, Tom Maloney wrote:

> Twenty years ago Edward Weston received the first Guggenheim Fellowship to be awarded a photographer. In the intervening years… the list of photographers who have received Fellowships could hardly be more impressive than it is. (Maloney 1958: 89)

Previous fellows had included Ansell Adams, Walker Evans, Dorothea Lange (the only woman), W. Eugene Smith and John Szarkowski. The Guggenheim fellowship would allow Frank to realize his hopes and follow his 'vision'. He was recommended for the award by Alexey Brodovitch, Alexander Lieberman, Edward Steichen, Meyer Schapiro and Walker Evans. Evans wrote:

> Dear Mr. Moe, It will be a pleasure to write of Robert Frank. The man is probably the most gifted of the younger photographers today. Anyway I think he is. I know his work quite well, and I know the man sufficiently to recommend him without reservation for a fellowship. Robert Frank is a born photographer if there is such a thing. Say he is a born artist, who

> has added to his natural gift of eye by thought, practice and study with the miniature camera. At the age he has now reached he has become an extremely serious (not solemn) worker of impressive depth of mind. The chief gift I speak of is imagination, and it is backed by the gift, or curse, of sensitivity. And rare is the man working in photography who is thus equipped… My point is that Robert Frank is working full blast in photography, and I'd like to see him encouraged.
>
> As to Frank's application project, I would trust him to produce really valuable work on an American trip. I think he has presented you with a plan knowingly designed to give himself scope. Selection will be his difficult problem, but he can do it. (Evans 1955, in Greenough 2009: 152)

Frank secured the grant, and later acknowledged his satisfaction with it and the way in which it allowed him to work:

> I am grateful to the Guggenheim Foundation for their confidence and the provisions they made for me to work freely in my medium over a protracted period. When I applied for the Guggenheim Fellowship, I wrote 'to produce an authentic contemporary document, the visual impact should be such as will nullify explanation'. (Frank, in Maloney 1958: 115)

All of these experiences and decisions led eventually to the man in the front seat of a car, pressing down the accelerator and heading out into the unknown. Jack Kerouac perhaps best describes how that moment might have felt:

> I pictured myself in a Denver bar that night, with all the gang, and in their eyes I would be strange and ragged and like the prophet who has walked across the land to bring the dark Word and the only Word I had was 'Wow!' (Kerouac 1972: 37)

A Guggenheim-sponsored, successful New York-based photographer set off in an attempt to push the boundaries of himself and his work. He would succeed:

> 1955. I cross the States. For a year. 500 rolls of film. I go into post offices, Woolworths, 10 cent shops, bus stations. I sleep in cheap hotels. Around 7 in the morning I go to a nearby bar. I work all the time. I don't speak much. I try not to be seen. One day in Arkansas the police stop me.

> What are you doing here?
> I have a Guggenheim Scholarship.
> Who's Guggenheim?
>
> I spent three days in prison. Anguish (Frank 1991: after plate 63)

The tools

As is so often the case, Frank's search for a more genuine way of working and of living was accompanied by the development of new working practices. Frank's arrival and experience in America was the occasion for a major change in his equipment and approach. In his European work, he had favoured a larger format Rolleiflex camera. Alexei Brodovitch championed the Leica camera to Frank while he was working for him at *Harper's Bazaar*:

> Brodovitch had encouraged me to shift to the Leica. I took both the cameras, the Rolleiflex and the Leica, to Peru, and I shifted to the 35mm in Peru. (Frank, in Johnson 1989: 30)

Louis Faurer confirms this in his recollection:

> I saw the Leica for the first time when Robert had it in 1947… I think I saw Robert's 35mm work at that time. The photographs from Switzerland were in a larger format. (Livingston 1992: 360)

This interest in the smaller format camera was not unusual. Lou Silverstein, art director of *The New York Times*, who worked with Frank for many years, commented later:

> A lot of things that Robert supposedly did at the time were part of a whole movement. (In the 1940s) the 35mm, available light thing happened. The lenses got faster, the film got faster and 35mm itself became popular. (Silverstein, in Brookman and Brookman 1986: video)

Many people opposed this movement. Berenice Abbott, for example, said to Allen Ginsberg:

> …all these photographers stand around going snap, snap, snap with their little cameras, they think they can get something. But you have to have a big format if you want minute detail in a big space. (Ginsberg, in Brookman and Brookman 1986: video)

From the perspective of Frank's work, this misses the point: 'minute detail' was not what Frank was after.

The film and lenses with which Frank worked were very different in quality to those used today. Sid Kaplan, who printed Frank's photographs from the late 1960s on, believes the nature of his film and lenses was important:

> The way he plays with light is beautiful. I don't know if one could describe the way it comes through the window, over-exposed, making all those little flares and haloes. A lot of it was probably exaggerated at the time because of the quality of the lenses that were produced. I don't think you could get it with the new lenses, because they're super-coated and multi-coated to get rid of all that. Shooting today with the new equipment you could go out and get a lens thirty years old, but another thing is the film. They've refined the film so much with all these super good anti-halation backings that even if you got one of those lenses, they've corrected the film so the light would never flair out. So that sense of light he got was partly due to the hardware and whatever kind of film was available at the time. (Kaplan, in Brookman and Brookman 1986: video)

Philip Brookman adds that Frank used a broken lens for some of his *contre jour* photographs, and that the higher silver content of photographic paper during the 1950s accounts for some of the quality of his work (Livingston 1992: 307).

The role played by technological innovations in artistic effort should not be underplayed. The Impressionist painters' search for the truth of a moment in light and colour was facilitated by the development and marketing of paint in tubes, enabling for the first time easy *plein air* painting. The technology abetted and facilitated the artists' purposes. So the 'miniature camera', as the 35mm Leica was described, and 35mm film facilitated *The Americans*.

Frank exploited the nature of the film, lenses and paper available to him, certainly, but this was in the service of his vision. The 35mm and its attendant limitations and possibilities represented an appropriate technical analogue to Frank's vision. They allowed him to wander inconspicuously around America and capture its secret moments, generally without being observed himself. As the Cubists painted with 'conceptual light' illuminating their work, a light from within their imaginations, so Frank exploited his equipment in order to paint his images with a light whose flares and haloes speak to his viewers' inner vision, not merely to the purely mechanical functions of their eyes. Frank comments generally on his use of black and white film soon after the publication of *The Americans* in an article in *Aperture*:

> Black and white are the colors of photography. To me they symbolize the alternatives of hope and despair to which mankind is forever subjected. (Frank 1961: 22)

Note

1. Not everyone was positive about the New York scene. William Klein said:

   > '…I didn't even live in New York, so there was a photographic establishment I wasn't a part of. The thing with Steichen at the Museum of Modern Art, the atmosphere around Brodovitch—I had no patience with that sort of thing. It didn't interest me. The other thing—*Life*, photographers in trenchcoats and with assistants—that didn't interest me either.' (Livingston 1992: 360)

3

A Divided World: 'Art' and 'Documentary' Photography

Les Americaines was published by Robert Delpire in 1958. This juxtaposed Frank's images with texts by various writers, chosen by Alain Bosquet. The first American edition, published by Grove Press in 1960,[1] saw 83 of Frank's images presented without text, instead having a simple caption describing the location of the shot. The only text was an introduction by Jack Kerouac. The photographs were immediately recognized as a radical departure from Frank's early work. Gotthard Schuh, a photographer friend from Switzerland, wrote the text for an article appearing in *Camera* in August 1957, featuring seventeen photographs, some of them later to be used in *The Americans*. He commented:

> I should never have thought that I could be so dismayed by your latest achievement, the fruits of your two-year stay in America … How little remains in these views of what we knew and loved in your previous work! No smile, no vegetation, no beauty, but only tormented, stolid human faces … I do not know America, but your pictures frighten me on account of the visionary watchfulness with which you depict things that concern us all. (Schuh 1957: 339–40)

Something in Frank's work had changed, leaving his old style behind and achieving something new. What was this and how did it happen? Frank describes his earlier work in Paris:

> To think that I was drawn to the very ordinary life in the streets and parks of Paris. Paris was very romantic and I was very romantic. From 1948 to 1950 I got that sentimentality out of my system, the pleasing photograph that has a kind of atmosphere. (Frank, in Johnson 1989: 32)

So much of his previous work was 'romantic', 'the pleasing photograph' with 'a kind of atmosphere'. Frank would acknowledge the importance of two photographers in particular in his development of *The Americans*. Comparing his earlier work to theirs is telling. Bill Brandt's *The English at Home* (1936) relates interestingly to images taken by Frank in Caereu, Wales in 1951, recording life amongst the town's miners. While Brandt presents a biting and eloquent social critique, cutting through the surfaces and deconstructing social relationships, Frank presents us with frontal images of the worthy and noble miners and their smiling children. Similarly, the children in Frank's *Paris, Porte de Clignancourt* (1949, collection of R. Delpire) are pictured contentedly playing a game.

Walker Evans' *Parked Car, Small Town Main Street* of 1932 (estate of W. Evans) is a photograph of a couple sitting in a car. Frank's *Paris, 1950* echoes both the subject and the look of Evans' picture. The difference, though, is that while the young people in Evans' picture frown, Frank's couple is laughing. It as if Frank is looking for *bonhomie*, wishing to reflect a certain gentility. Like much of Cartier-Bresson's work, Frank's early observations are usually made with a wry smile. A superb example is his record of smiling girls in a diner in New York, taken in 1951. A subject that he would examine with the utmost care and critical precision in *The Americans* is here presented as a jolly, frontal portrait.

This gentility is characteristic of the 'art' photography ethos of the 50s. Edward Steichen, in his famous *The Family of Man* exhibition, dealt with issues like war, poverty and disease, but held back from including the most powerful figurations of these subjects. The image of a fallen GI used in the exhibition is a useful example (R. Platnick, *Eniwetok*, undated, archive of the US Coastguard). It shows flawless skin beneath a ripped shirt. There is no blood, only the body's sprawl and an impaled rifle, standing sentinel, define this as death. Steichen's own *After the Taking of Iwo Jima* (1943, Museum of Modern Art, New York) describes war dead with an eloquence vastly more wrenching than the photograph he selected for the exhibition.

Steichen, perhaps reflecting his membership of the *Photo Secession*, the American group dedicated to the propagation of photographic art, appears to have believed that overly violent or contentious images were not consistent with 'art'. Whenever an image in his exhibition threatened to be political or controversial, he subverted it with an accompanying text. There is an insistence on gentility. Walker Evans, in his *Introduction* to Frank's photographs in the *US Camera Annual of* 1958, described Steichen's exhibition off-handedly as 'woolly, successful, "photo sentiments" about human familyhood' (Evans, in Maloney 1958: 90).

Gentility was a constant companion in the work of gallery oriented 'art' photographers at the time. Edward Weston's superb still lives of peppers and shells, and his beautifully composed and realized nudes, exist alongside Ansell Adams' celebrated records of Yosemite and the work of his f64 group colleagues in an almost conceptual world, idealised, declining warts or ugliness. Alexei Brodovitch's *Ballet* (1945) similarly features misty, fine-figured dancers wearing filigree tutus in a staged world. The photographs of New York taken by colleagues and friends of Frank during this time play with composition, focus, distortion and reflection, yet none has the sting of Jacob Riis' earlier unschooled works, which aimed to educate and change society.

Frank, as has been noted, was part of this world, working for Brodovitch and travelling and contributing to Steichen's shows. His gentility is not entirely surprising. We have noted that Robert grew up as a middle-class Jew in Zurich. He had been successful in his chosen profession from the start and quickly found high-profile work when he arrived in New York. He had been aware, of course, of the constant threat from Nazi Germany during the war, and had travelled quite extensively afterwards through a Europe bearing its scars. He was certainly no stranger to poverty or privation, as his Caereu and Bolivian photographs testify; however, as with the *Family of Man*, there is an optimism in the eye behind the lens, a bright side looking on.

All American photography was certainly not genteel. There was influential and eloquent work that entirely eschewed it. Many significant and powerful photographs of American experience are well known. The stunning images made by Jacob Riis mentioned above are an example. His *Twelve-year-old boy (who had sworn he was sixteen) pulling threads in a sweat shop* (Riis 1890: 99) reveals, without words, the desperate plight of this vulnerable, beaten and abused child in the midst of his smiling tormentors. The genius of the work is the recording of the brutality of this scene with the full and jovial consent of the very people whose actions he is lambasting. His *Bandit's Roost* (Riis 1890: 51), similarly, is a more biting and unsettling evocation of the brutality of gang dominated ghetto life than anything Hollywood has since offered. Weegee's shockingly graphic pictures of murder victims include his *Murder in Hell's Kitchen* (1940, Galerie Berinson, Berlin). This composition slowly carries the viewer from a man's face lying on the pavement, to the hole in his cheek, to the pool of blood seemingly coagulated around his prostrate form. A gun, presumably the murder weapon, points at the corpse, leaving no doubt as to the image's meaning. All of this lit by exactly enough light from Weegee's flash. William Dyviniak's *Car Accident, Cheektowaga* (1945, collection of Wide World) records its lifeless victim hanging high above the road in a mess of telegraph wires. This tragic subject is echoed in the harshly delineated, flash lit white on black of the image. I. Russell Sorgi's *Suicide* (1942, collection of Buffalo Courier Express) records, astoundingly, a falling woman moments before she hits the stone pavement. The powerful verticals of the city block and streets heighten the stolid solidity of the material world, which the woman in this image has chosen to deny.

These images powerfully capture moments and offer them up for perusal. There is comment, too, in all of these images: they are not victims of the nonsensical notions of photographic objectivity. In Weegee, there is a palpable sense of his pleasure in the strange beauty of the accidental composition on the pavement. Dyviniak's picture is a slap in the face from the happenchance of existence, an Absurdist document rendered infinitely potent by its reality. Sorgi's image is offered as a celebration of the miraculous, a moment beyond any possible planning or expectation, caught in a camera.

All of these images are documentary photojournalism. They were not included in MOMA's exhibitions, and no one pushed them forward as 'art'. Frank was no stranger to the notion of the photograph as document. His portfolio *40 Fotos* included studio photographs of industrially produced objects, and reportage images of parades and aspects of everyday life (albeit expressed with gentility!). Equally, his images from *Indiens Pas Morts* communicate as much through their compositions as they do through their subject matter. However, to claim that he lost his gentility because he followed the photojournalists and adopted a 'documentary' approach is too simplistic.

An interesting clue to the reasons for the changes in Frank's work, which were observed by Shuh, lies in a letter Frank sent to his parents: 'America is an interesting country but there is a lot here that I do not like and I would never accept. I am trying to show this in my photos.' (Frank 1955, in Tucker and Brookman 1986: 28) Frank needed a form for his expression, something that would reflect his feelings about the country and the people he was experiencing. T.S. Eliot calls it the objective correlative, the form that fits its content (Eliot 1932). Writing after his journey's conclusion, Frank acknowledged that new influences had taken over: 'The work of two contemporary photographers, Bill Brandt of England and Walker Evans of America have influenced me.' (Frank in Maloney 1958: 115) Significantly, there is no more mention of Steichen or Brodovitch.

What do Brandt and Evans have that is so critical to the development of Frank's work? Brandt's *The English at Home* (1936), which we mentioned above, comments on the society it is observing by its juxtaposition of upper- and working-class English experiences. This is often achieved by his selection of 'moments', capturing in the expressions of his subjects their attitudes to the scenarios he is recording. Further, Brandt threads his images together to form a whole, with each individual image serving an overall communication of opinion.

Walker Evans' *American Photographs* (1938) similarly identifies moments and objects that, in their particularity, describe and exemplify the America through which he was travelling, and within which he was existing. His work is very different to Brandt's, speaking about precision, a passionate interest in the details of the collisions of form and tone captured with an icy detachment. Evans is always powerfully present in his images.[2]

Brandt and Evans have a message to convey. They are not afraid of losing their gentility or of exceeding the assumptions about 'art' photography to do it. At the same time, though, their sustained complexity, their planned and considered accumulation and deployment of images, exceed standard notions about reportage photography. Weegee, Dyviniak and Sorgi are reactive in comparison, lacking calculation and consideration. They are serendipitous: their intention is to effectively record the moment. Brandt and Evans don't only record what they see, they also have something to say. A crucial difference, then, is the notion of intent or purpose.

Brandt, Evans and Frank, while eschewing the gentility associated with art photography, retain notions of structure, communication, commitment and message that are often associated with the notions of 'art'. Their works, at the same time, have more intention than is consistent with the production of reportage work. This compromises attempts to describe them as 'documentary'. They bring these approaches together, finding the hugely fertile common ground between them. In venturing into this place, exploring these possibilities, they achieve something else. Frank confirms his interest in this hinterland in his application for Guggenheim funding:

> This project is essentially the visual study of a civilization…but it is only partly documentary in nature: one of its aims is more artistic than the word documentary implies. (Frank, in Tucker and Brookman 1986: 20)

Having eschewed documentary 'purity', Frank nonetheless retains and exhibits something of the search for visual lucidity, clarity of communication and self-containment that characterizes the best of America's reportage works. As he combines the uncowed depiction of the sometimes unpalatable truth with his personal 'artistic' intention, so he adds message and intent to the austerity of the photojournalist.

Interestingly, John Szarkowski, another Guggenheim fellowship recipient and later curator of photography at MOMA, New York, had previously described Walker Evans' *American Photographs* as 'hard to take'. (Szarkowski, in Livingston 1992: 308). He said something similar about Frank's book:

> I saw it I suppose very shortly after it was published, when I was still working as a photographer myself, and it was, frankly, shocking. I sensed the power in it, and the authority about it but there was much about it that I didn't like…*The Americans* was received with mixed critical reaction. Not primarily because of its subject matter, although many people thought so at the time. There had been many people who clearly disliked it or hated it. Looking back on it now, if you analyze the subject matter of *The Americans*, it in fact is subject matter that has been recorded, described with considerable depth by a good many other photographers. It was something in the very bones of the photographs themselves—something about the look of the pictures that suggested that, whereas what was being described had to be described because it was there, it didn't have to be described according to the rules and formulations that were thought of as being good photography… We all knew those things existed … but

> the way in which they were depicted made them seem more difficult to accept, more pessimistic. There was something approaching a sharp edge of bitterness in the look of the pictures. And of course what was eventually learned from that was that it was not necessarily the sensibility that gave the pictures their bitter taste, but rather the knowledge that the medium itself was much more plastic, and was open to a wider range of invention than we ever realized. (Szarkowski, in Brookman and Brookman 1986: video)

Szarkowski suggests that there is something in the 'very bones of the photographs … approaching a sharp edge of bitterness' and that 'the medium was much more plastic, and was open to a wider range of invention than we ever realised'. He is recognizing the destruction, in Frank's photographs, of the association of gentility and art photography. He is describing the uncomfortable and challenging reaction of many viewers to the maturation of the form. Frank, it seems, found his form, his 'objective correlative'.[3]

All of this uniting of disparate traditions and the extension of the possibilities and range of 'art' photography is not sufficient as an explanation of Frank's remarkable achievement. It is the power and particularity of his vision that is pivotal. He wrote:

> There is one thing the photograph must contain, the humanity of the moment. This kind of photography is realism. But realism is not enough—there has to be vision, and the two together can make a good photograph. (Frank 1961: 22)

and: 'The view is personal.' (Frank, in Maloney 1958: 115)

Frank's personal vision forms the subject of Parts Two and Three of this work. Jack Kerouac celebrates the power of the vision in his valedictory Introduction to *The Americans*: 'Anybody doesn't like these pitchers don't like potry see?' and:

> with that little camera that he raises and snaps with one hand he sucked a sad poem right out of America onto film, taking rank among the tragic poets of the world. To Robert Frank I now give this message: You got eyes. (Kerouac, in Frank 1959: 6)

Kerouac is confirming Frank's achievement. His poetic and prophetic eye ranged over America and captured images of such particularity and quality that they constitute for Kerouac a 'sad poem' of world class. This 'poetry' is the heart of *The American*'s success. The work's sadness is the soft sadness of melancholy rather than that of tragedy; it is a sadness born of compassion rather than bitterness. Frank wrote:

> I have been frequently accused of deliberately twisting subject matter to my point of view. Above all I know that life for a photographer cannot be a matter of indifference. Opinion often consists of a kind of criticism. But criticism can come out of love. (Frank, in Maloney 1958: 115)

Notes

1. Although the Grove Press edition is dated 1959, it was actually released in January 1960.

2. There are others worthy of mention. Writer Erskine Caldwell and photographer Margaret Bourke-White's book *You Have Seen Their Faces* (1937) was similarly more than a record. It was a manifesto, declaring its creators' opinions, seeking engagement from its viewers and soliciting change. Frank also acknowledges the influence of Kertesz and Faurer (Johnson 1989: 29–30)

3. Willem de Kooning, as we have noted, insisted that photography was an art form equal to painting. Painting, drawing, music and so many other manifestations of the notion of 'art' have eschewed gentility and engaged with ugliness, brutality and death for as long as such objects and actions have existed. In terms contemporary to Frank, we can cite Pablo Picasso's *Guernica* (1937, Museo Reina Sofia, Madrid), de Kooning's own *Woman* series (1950–52, Museum of Modern Art, New York) and Francis Bacon's *Figures at the Foot of the Crucifix* (1944, Tate, London), all easily accessible at the time. Frank's images in *The Americans* evidence the truth of de Kooning's assessment of equality.

4

The Creation, Selection and Programming of *The Americans*' Images: All That Jazz

During his two-year journey across the United States, Frank took a vast number of photographs. He says in his autobiographical notes for the *Photofile Robert Frank* that he took 500 rolls of film (1991: after plate 45). Anne Tucker (Tucker and Brookman 1986: 90) argues that the contact sheets for *The Americans* are numbered 1 to 751, followed by a new system for Frank's later photographs of the Democratic Convention. This suggests that '500' was a rough approximation. Sarah Greenough, who has had unrivalled access to Frank's archive material, suggests that precise allocation of images to the Guggenheim work is problematic, due to the various projects in which Frank was involved, but suggests that there were at least 767 rolls of film (Greenough 2009: 133 and 376). Frank had made it clear in his initial Fellowship application that his 'total production will be voluminous, as is usually the case with miniature film' (Frank 1954 in Greenough 2009: 362).

We've examined something of the motivations behind the taking of his photographs, Frank's search for 'the black and white, the knowledge of where God is' (1991: after plate 63). What about the individual photographs? Why did he choose to capture these particular images as against all the myriad other possibilities? What guided his hand and eye as he checked his contact sheets, produced work prints and then made his final selection?

There are some clues. He said after he had finished *The Americans*:

> I continue to look around me, but I am no longer the solitary observer… Instead I'm trying to recapture what I saw, what I heard and what I feel. What I know! There is no decisive moment. It's got to be created. (Frank 1991: after plate 45)

Frank described himself as a 'solitary observer' during the making of *The Americans*: 'I don't speak much. I try not to be seen.' (1991: 45) He is clearly suggesting that at the time the 'Decisive Moment' notion was significant for him. The 'Decisive Moment' was photographer Henri Cartier-Bresson's idea. He wrote:

> ...inside movement there is one moment at which the elements in motion are in balance. Photography must seize upon this moment and hold immobile the equilibrium of it...Composition...at the moment of shooting can stem only from our intuition for we are out to capture the fugitive moment and all the interrelationships are on the move. (Cartier-Bresson 1952: 50)[1]

Cartier-Bresson's idea is that we look for a moment of balance, of 'rightness', when we know intuitively, in an instant of clarity, that something in the arrangement of time and space, for that second only, reaches deep into who we are and resonates with us. It is a powerful argument and has been hugely influential.

The look of many of Frank's Guggenheim Fellowship photographs certainly suggests that they were taken rapidly, as if Frank were snatching at something, desperately trying to catch a moment before it was gone. He was clearly 'attempting to capture the fugitive moment' but he differs from Bresson with regard to equilibrium. Many of his evening and indoor images are out of focus. His selection of these photographs for inclusion reveals a preference for the flawed record of a moment over technical perfection. His *modus operandi* in these works relates, interestingly, to the techniques used by the painters with whom he lived and socialized. Many of them were interested in 'gestural painting', as practised most famously by Jackson Pollock, in which the hand, paint, canvas, intellect and imagination conspire to create and communicate. This approach has similarities to jazz improvisation, living creatively within the moment while being always aware of the structure into which that moment's responses fit. John Szarkowski called Frank's photographs 'casual, almost offhand' (Livingston 1992: 308). We could equally well describe them as 'gestural photography', with the photograph being the response to a moment, an improvisation within the structure of the overall project's plan. Frank was grasping for the moment, flicking his camera in an attempt to capture something before it was gone, just as surely as Pollock was manipulating his brush. A remark from Kerouac provides a first-hand observation of Frank's technique: 'that little camera that he raises and snaps with one hand' (Kerouac, in Frank 1959: 6).

Frank also departs from Bresson in his subordination of the individual photograph's 'moment' to his overall intention. The wonderful images left out of *The Americans* testify to this: Frank created the book by looking at what he had and seeing where it could go. He said:

> I think that trip was almost pure intuition. I just kept on photographing. I kept on looking. I think at that time I was compassionate. I had a feeling of compassion for the people on the street. That was the main meat of the book—that gave me the push—that made me work so hard until I knew that I had something but I didn't even know I had America. (Frank, in Wheeler 1977: 22)

These technically imperfect images were chosen and included because they caught the exact and most appropriate moment of communication, the moment when 'matter ends and mind begins' (Frank 1961: 22). This was more important than a beautiful print.

Frank's vision in *the Americans* was specific:

> With these photographs, I have attempted to show a cross-section of the American population. My effort was to express it simply and without confusion. The view is personal (Frank, in Maloney 1958: 115)

Frank searches for the communication of his simple, personal vision in his selection and preparation of photographs.

City Fathers – Hoboken, New Jersey is a useful exemplar of the process through which Frank appears to have gone. It is *The Americans*' second image, which signals its significance. The contact sheet (Greenough 2009: 379) shows several takes of the same scene: a group of politicians on a dais. We might call this 'speculative photography', reaching for something, sensing that there is something important there, some potential, hoping that it might reveal itself to the lens without really knowing exactly what it is, or even exactly what one is hoping for.

The shot before the one eventually chosen (frame 27 on the contact) is rather busy. The eye wanders aimlessly; there is no clear compositional focus. The most attractive visual element is a large tricolour rosette. The photograph ringed in red crayon (frame 28), which was selected, moves the previously dominant rosette down, placing it a fifth of the way up from the base of the photograph, along a golden section line. The heads of the row of politicians are no longer cut off, creating space in the image. They occupy the centre band, focusing our attention on them. The upward rake of their heads leads the eye towards the enigmatic expression of the man at the extreme right, making him the subject of the photograph. Frank has cropped the image for every edition of *The Americans*, always removing the head of a politician to the right (Greenough 2009: 461) in order to heighten this focus and amplify the aspects of his 'personal vision' which the photograph embodies.

So what has Frank's personal vision fixed on in this picture, what is the story that he is so keen to tell? The politicians' top-hatted pomp is juxtaposed with their stolid bored expressions. There is a supporting character in the image, playing a subsidiary role. He is second from right and characterizes the corrupt, power-hungry mandarin, dismissive of the event, not even dressed for the occasion. He could be Joseph Kennedy, Randolph Hearst or any one of Hollywood's depictions of the dark world of American politics. Richard Nixon was Vice President at this time, a man who could suitably be invoked here. The man at extreme right, though, is the focus of the image. His expression is incongruous and unexpected. Is he praying? Blowing a kiss? If so, to whom? The overwhelming impression is of arrogance, confident defiance and self-satisfaction. It is a distinctly 'kiss my ass' gesture. Jack Kerouac, in his introduction to *The Americans*, recognized that the picture's importance lay in the capturing of this particular moment. He described it as:

> Hoboken in the winter, platform full of politicians all ordinary looking till suddenly at the far end to the right you see one of them pursing his lips in prayer politico (yawning probably) not a soul cares. (Kerouac, in Frank 1959: 2)

The expression of the politician was the necessary element, supported by a composition that draws the eye towards the enigma. *City Fathers - Hoboken, New Jersey* captured something of the particular kind of 'decisive moment' that Frank was seeking, a moment which was manipulated and included in order to communicate Frank's vision.

As is so often the case, a comparison with other contemporary photographs—of which Frank was certainly aware—can extend our understanding. Steichen's *The Family of Man* exhibition depicted American officials in a sharply contrasting way. There they are depicted as heroes, the guardians and perhaps even the saviours of the modern world. Bob Schwalberg's *Beat Policeman* (collection of Pix) and Dan Weiner's photograph of an American judge (collection of Brackman Associates) are juxtaposed with a quotation from Sir Thomas Noon Talfourd: 'fill the seats of justice with good men, not so absolute in goodness as to forget human frailty' (Steichen 1955: 172). These photographs imply a faith in the American system and its stalwarts, even accounting for the all too well-known corruption in a positive manner. Frank illustrates instead the real frailty of which Talfourd speaks, presenting a personal view, identifiably different from Steichen's, simply and without confusion.

City Fathers – Hoboken, New Jersey is a successful single image. Its communication is extended significantly, however, when it is considered alongside the image that precedes it. Philip Brookman says (Coke and Du Pont 1986: 124) that *City Fathers* was taken during a parade, linking it intimately with *Parade – Hoboken, New Jersey*, which comes before. This is *The Americans*' opening image, and features two figures standing in the upper-storey windows of a building, with an American flag between them. It is a depiction of unknown people, shown in this image as literally faceless. They stand for the legion unknown Americans who fuelled and fed the industrial development of their country. For all their living and dying, this faceless portrait will be their most notable memorial. Anonymous, obscured by the billowing stars and stripes, the stories and lives of these flesh-and-blood women are hidden somewhere in America. This is a powerful foil to the self-satisfied politicos whom the page's turn will reveal.

This link is important, picking up as it does one of the book's abiding themes: the juxtaposition of unknown and insignificant poor Americans with their more eminent and well-heeled countrymen. Frank described this as 'the faces of the leaders and the faces of the followers' in his Guggenheim application (Frank, in Greenough 2009: 362). These images also demonstrate another of Frank's interests: looking and being watched. He said: 'The first four or five pictures are of people looking, spectators. And then you see what they're looking at' (Frank, in Alexander 1997: 38).

This powerful pairing of images clearly echoes Bill Brandt's practice in *The English at Home*, as we have seen. Frank was not, though, wedded to this notion of diptychs. *The Americans* often presents extended series of linked images, and even at times includes images that do not discernibly relate to their adjacent photographs. *Parade – Hoboken, New Jersey* and *City Fathers – Hoboken, New Jersey* are a thematically linked pair, but they are also part of an extended series of related adjacent images. This series is characterized by the representation of gesture. The flag-obscured lady on the right hand side of *Parade* holds her hand to her mouth in a gesture that looks like uncertainty. The hatted politician in *City Fathers* makes a gesture of opposition, sharing none of her ambivalence and pursing his lips in the supremely confident gesture discussed above. The subject of the next photograph, *Political Rally, Chicago*, holds wide his arms, his fists clenched, his mouth open and his eyes closed in an abandoned declamation, it appears, of political fealty. Following him, a pensive black man looks quietly on in *Funeral, St Helena, South Carolina*. He too is holding his hand to his mouth, a gesture echoed by the man in a lighter suit behind him and the man to his left. The gravity of their remembrance of a life lived and over is held in their contemplative gestures. They are followed by an image of a tall, white man in an oversize Western hat. He is contemplative too, and again holds his hand to his chin. His contemplation is of something off to the photograph's right. His expression is serious, certainly, but lacks the sombre tones of the preceding image. The caption of the photograph reveals the reason for his attention: *Rodeo: Detroit*. He is smoking a cigar, which leads us into the next image, also of a cigar smoker, as Frank dispenses with gesture as his linking thread.

So, then, the book's complexity is becoming apparent. The opening image can be read firstly as itself, secondly as part of a thematically linked pair and thirdly as part of a short series of visually related adjacent images. It doesn't, of course, end there. Frank decided early on to divide his book into four parts, beginning each part with a photograph of the American flag (Frank, in Alexander 1997: 38). The other section-heading flags are in plates 17, 37 and 58. The American flag reappears throughout the book, which gives us the fifth and last set to which *Parade Hoboken* belongs: the extended, complex and sophisticated consideration of the iconography of the American flag.

Not everyone accepts this reading of Frank's *The Americans*. The idea of visual structures and notions of narrative in purely visual work may be widely accepted, but there are those who do not accept that Frank's work was created with this in mind, or functions in this way. Ulrich Keller, for example, called the book an 'impatient sequence of irreverent photographs' and 'a catalogue of irritations' (Keller 1986: 23). In a comparison between Frank's work and efforts undertaken for Standard Oil, he wrote:

> The fact is that much of the Standard Oil archive was conceived in terms of sequences, or stories rather than individual works (or as the case may be, collections of such works in book form). When put in narrative sequence, explaining and supporting each other, the pictures become capable of something special and unparalleled in Frank's oeuvre: i.e. the description of particular segments of the nation's social texture, of certain institutionalized phases of daily life, of the structure and flavor of vernacular pockets in the blander mainstream of American middle class existence. (Keller 1986: 43)

Keller does not recognize that Frank has a narrative sequence at all, much less that he is undertaking a 'description of particular segments of the nation's social texture', despite Frank stating at the outset that this was his purpose. Frank is too subtle and too sophisticated for Keller.

In further countering such criticisms, we should remember that Frank spent a year putting *The Americans* together, after the images had been taken. During the latter part of 1956, Frank finished developing his films. His huge Fellowship resource of perhaps 27,000 photographs was printed up as contact sheets and then initially reduced to perhaps 1000 work prints: I have seen prints numbered up to the mid-700s, so this is an estimation. These 8 by 10 inch proofs were numbered according to the order and date on the rolls of film (Livingston 1992: 305; Greenough 2009: 133). He then spread these on tables and the floor, and tacked and stapled them to his apartment walls in various sequences (Tucker and Brookman 1986: 95; Greenough 2009: 133). Given the time Frank spent selecting and sequencing his images, it is ludicrous to suggest that the result is 'impatient' or 'careless'. Frank himself said that this selection of approximately 100 from 1000 was 'the biggest job in that book' (Greenough 2009: 133). Nothing in Frank's past, either, suggests that this was his way.

The argument for *The Americans* as a considered, integrated and structured communication is further eloquently evidenced by the superb images that were left out of the work. It cannot be argued that Frank was blind to their qualities, as he exploited them elsewhere in books and exhibitions. Frank subordinated the individual quality of his photographs to his overall intention for the book. If Keller's assessment were correct, and *The Americans* is a series of 'individual works (or as the case may be, collections of such works in book form)' (Keller 1986: 43), then the exclusion of photographs that Frank and others rated highly would be inexplicable.

The notion of impatience is further brought into question by the nature of the project. *The Americans* was, from its inception, considered as a book. Frank made this aspect of the project clear in his initial funding application. We've already noted that the photo book was a desirable form since, although exhibitions and photo journals like *Camera* were prestigious, books gave an artist's work longevity. In book form, a photographer's work could remain accessible long after an exhibition had closed. Frank had already experimented with various structures in earlier books: he was no newcomer to the rigours of sequencing. His maquette for *Peru* (1949) was first organized by theme, cane cutting or market day for example, very much along the lines of the 'photo-essays' found in magazines. The final sequencing, however, presented the images in a less immediate way, communicating clearly Frank's desire to express ideas through his work. His unique book of photographs of Paris, created in 1949 for Mary Lockspeiser, who he would later marry, was organized diaristically around aspects of the city and himself. Significantly, *Black, White and Things*, 1952, the book that preceded *The Americans*, and that was made in collaboration with designer Werner Zyrd, was arranged in three sections. These followed the title. 'Black' was characterized as 'sombre people and black events', 'White' as 'quiet people and peaceful places' and 'Things' as 'things people have come in contact with' (Frank 1995: 3). Frank was placing his photographs into a preconceived narrative structure.

Most significant for Frank's structural design were the two books we have mentioned already in another context, and whose influence he acknowledged. These are Bill Brandt's *The English at Home*, published in 1936, and Walker Evans' *American Photographs* of 1938. The images in *Black, White and Things* were presented as linked pairs following Brandt's example, which commented on its images by their juxtaposition. The misty, tree-spattered valley of *November in the Country*, for example, is contrasted with the precise geometry of the rain-wet roofs of *November in the Suburbs* (both 1936, estate of B. Brandt). These thematic couplings are accompanied by visually linked pairs such as *A Meet of the Foxhounds* and *A London Pasture: Hampstead Heath* (1936, estate of B. Brandt), both of which are taken from a similarly low viewpoint and feature a group of animals resting on grass, in front of a tree-lined horizon. *Black, White and Things* adopted this method, juxtaposing *Men of Wood* (1952, collection of the artist) for example, a picture of a wooden statue of Christ in a procession in Malaga, with a photograph of a hand holding religious medals. An old woman selling cigarettes on the roadside in Barcelona is similarly contrasted with a *Parisienne* in a skin-tight white dress, linking them by gender while contrasting them through notions of age, culture and circumstance. As we have see, Frank acknowledged the influence of Brandt in the Statement that accompanied some of his Fellowship photographs in the 1958 *US Camera Annual* (Maloney 1958: 115). There is another link: *The English at Home* was created by a German-born photographer closely associated with England, as *The Americans* was created by a Swiss-born photographer closely associated with America.

Significantly, and despite the frequent articulations between sequentially associated images, Frank does not follow Brandt's example of facing pairs in *The Americans*. Instead, Frank's images are presented one at a time, with each photograph facing a blank page carrying a caption. This was the style of Walker Evans' *American Photographs*. Walker Evans was very important to Frank. He said of him:

> Walker had a stronger influence on me than his pictures did. He wasn't a phony; he was very intelligent and uncompromising. He had class and style. It was an education for me to work for him. He was my teacher. I learned a lot from the way that he looked at things; he wanted to look at one thing and look at it very clearly and in a final way. I like that about him because I don't have that…and also he wouldn't put up with any shit or give any shit. (Johnson 1989: 35)

Evans' *American Photographs* is the closest pattern for *The Americans*, presenting its images on the right-hand folio, faced by a blank page. This presentation is important for the multilayered significance of the images within the book, since it preserves the integrity of the individual image, allowing it to be assessed and understood as a particular moment. Abandoning the paired presentation allows the pictures to refer forwards and backwards into both adjacent and distant images within the book.

There is, then, clear seriousness and intelligence behind the sequencing of *The Americans'* images. The selection and inclusion of images is as much about their place and function within the book as it is about their individual qualities. *The Americans* is clearly not structured in an immediate or transparent manner, since several writers fail to see any structure in it at all. What, then, is the nature of Frank's structuring? How can his intentions be demonstrated and described? The key is in Frank's rejection, along with so many other creatives of the Modernist era, of the linear narrative structures so popular and time-honoured within Western culture.

The Americans departs radically from the traditional narrative style of the 'picture story' or 'photo-essay'. This approach was well established in the 1950s and widely used in magazines such as *Picture Post*, *Life* and *Look*. Photo-stories were usually arranged so that images served some kind of linguistic narrative. This was also often true of books and exhibitions: Steichen's *The Family of Man* is a good example. Roy Stryker, whose leadership of the Farm Security Administration's Photo Section and oversight of the Standard Oil Picture File make him a very significant figure in mid-twentieth century photography, saw the writing of the story as an essential preparation for a shoot. For Stryker, narrative structure should precede photography:

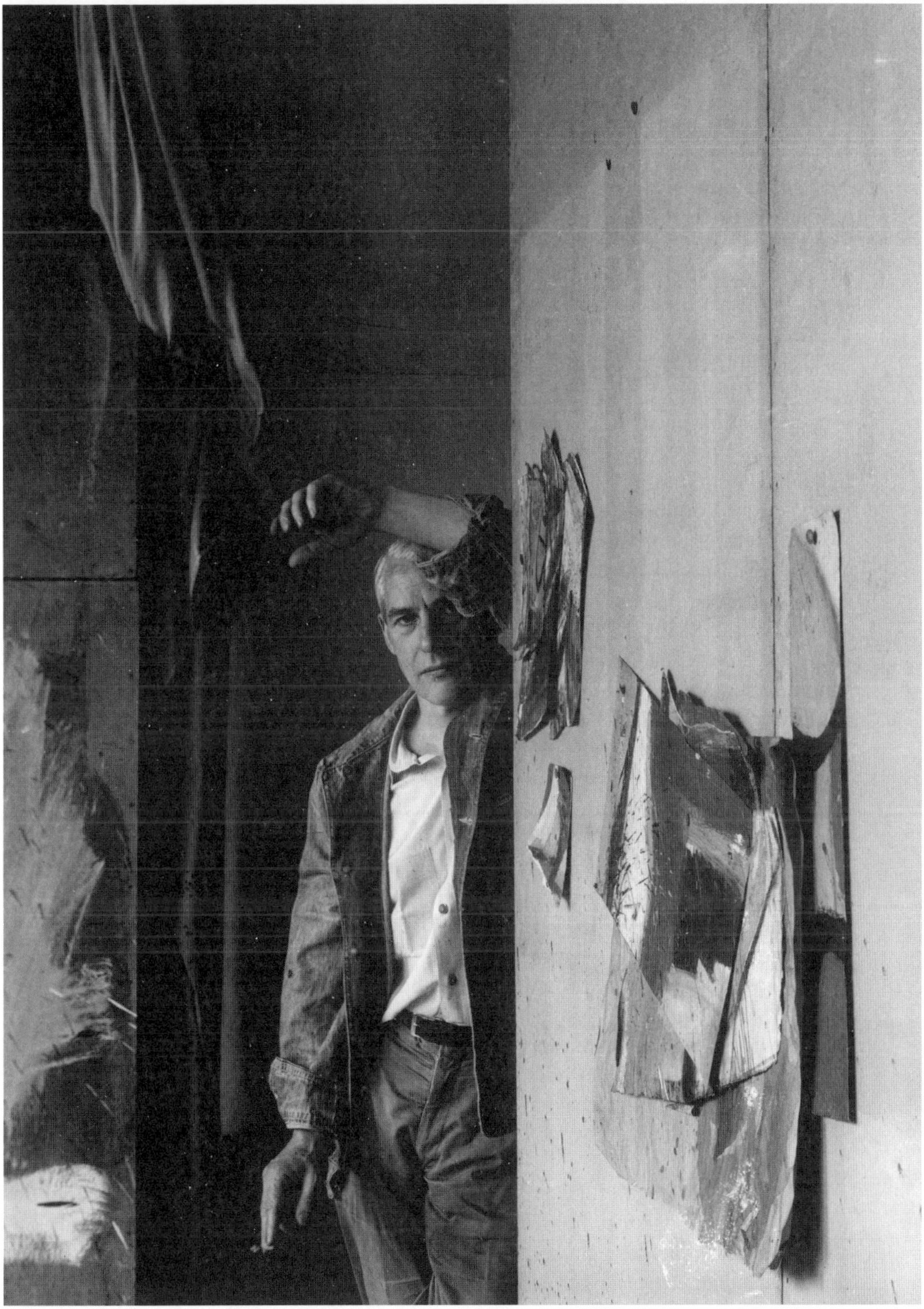

Willem de Kooning in his studio May 25th, 1959, New York City (Arnold Newman/Getty Images). Frank lived across the yard from de Kooning and was deeply impressed by the efforts he made in pursuit of his painting.

> Shooting scripts are the most important thing in the world. First of all you must analyse. You must be able to analyse your story and think the story out. Accidental photographs are not of consequence. (Stryker 1946: 133 and 138)

We've commented already on Frank's elevation of the notion of 'vision'. This is a description of an intention towards meaning on the part of the photographer, which precedes and informs the actual image-making. This might easily be compared to Stryker's notion of the script.[2] The difference is that Frank's 'script' was to find the essence of 'the black and white, of where God is' (Frank 1991: after plate 63). Such a poetic notion needs its perpetrator to be absolutely reflexive to his experiences. It requires, as a prerequisite, openness and uncertainty. Communicating the intuited and half-understood results of such an endeavour required more than the traditional photo story could accommodate.

Frank needed something different, a new way of constructing his work. Fortunately, there were examples of variant approaches all around him, even if these were not found in photographic practice. New York was, perhaps, the prime locus of the Western creative world during the 1950s. Its bookshops, coffee bars and galleries were filled with experimental writing, music and visuals. Frank and his family lived in an apartment on Third Avenue, near 9th Street, during the early 50s. This was a downtown bohemian neighbourhood at the time, and Frank had the painter Alfred Leslie as his next-door neighbour and Willem de Kooning was just across the yard. Frank has spoken about watching de Kooning through his window late at night and being impressed by how hard he had to work to create his paintings (Johnson 1989: 35):

> I think that the people that influenced me the most were the abstractionist painters I met; and what influenced me strongly was the way these painters lived in the 1940s and early 1950s. Their struggle, they were people who really believed in what they did… You live on 9th and 3rd and around you are painters and you watch what goes on. You are not a painter but it does something to you to be around them and watch how they believe in what they do. So it reinforced my belief that you could really follow your intuition—no matter how crazy or far-off or how laughed at it would be. You could go and make pictures that were not sentimental. You could photograph what you felt like. (Frank, in Johnson 1989: 36)

Experimentation with form and the rejection of linearity characterized much of the work in which Frank was immersed. Creative people were kicking against tradition, always looking for the 'new' and Modern, looking to move on from the past. This notion of movement, the perfectibility of humanity on its 'journey to the stars' is a key aspect of the Modernist world at whose heart Frank was standing.[3] The notion of narrative propriety was a cornerstone of the creative traditions that Frank's generation was challenging. These dominating ideas can be traced in the West at least as far back as Aristotle. In his *Poetics* (2003), he describes the necessary aspects of a successful plot. These include the 'Unity' of time, action, place and several others. Aristotle did not invent these ideas; rather, he identified and codified certain aspects of the nature of human storytelling; his own work was heavily based on observations of the plays of the long-dead Sophocles. There is no question that he was in many ways right, and most Western creative effort reflects these ideas. Perhaps the most significant aspect of Aristotle for Frank is his commentary on the 'narrative arc' (2003: 23). This asserts that a story must have a clearly delineated and articulated beginning, middle and end. Frank knowingly evokes this in his criticisms of magazine picture stories, especially those in *Life*:

> I wanted to sell my pictures to *Life* magazine and they never did buy them. So I developed a tremendous contempt for them…I also wanted to follow my own intuition and do it my way—not make a *Life* story. That was another thing I hated. Those god-damned stories with a beginning a middle and an end. (Janis and MacNeil 1977: 56)

Ideas around the destruction of linear form resulted, earlier in the century, in experiments with 'simultaneity' in the visual arts and 'stream of consciousness' in literature. European painters had collapsed and concertinaed time in response to observations and revelations emerging from the new sciences of psychology and psychiatry. In order to closer approximate the way our senses and minds interact, artists such as Umberto Boccioni, in his *Fusion of a Head and Window* (1912, destroyed, photograph in Clay 1978: 235), Gino Severini, in *Dynamic Hieroglyph of the Bal Tabarin* of 1912 (Museum of Modern Art, New York) and Kasimir Malevitch, in *An Englishman in Moscow* of 1913 (Stedelijk Museum, Amsterdam) had depicted aspects of experience slurred one across another. Temporally separated events and geographically distanced objects were brought into collision by consciousness in their works. These montages of apparently disassociated objects, cutting into and stuck over each other, are bewildering to our rational thinking and ask to be understood intuitively, betraying their import less readily than traditional narrative. James Joyce, in his novel *Ulysses* of 1922, attempted to write in a manner analogous to thinking. So-called 'stream-of-consciousness' writing records one image cutting into another in a barely ordered chaos of perception, memory and intention.[4]

Jack Kerouac, most tellingly, also departed from conventional practise in his so-called 'spontaneous prose'. He wrote the first draft of his novel *On the Road* in three weeks, an achievement which Truman Capote (soon to work with Avedon and Brodovitch) derided, saying: 'That isn't writing; it's typing.' (Charters in Kerouac 2007: 9) Kerouac's work is often close to 'stream of consciousness', and its structure is intuitive, improvisational and organic. It emerges from the passage of time. It flows out as a flawed recollection, a story with themes that submerge and surface like the whales Kerouac and so many others famously watched from the cliffs of Big Sur.

The questioning and destruction of linearity is also, and most significantly, evidenced in the creations and the aesthetics of jazz. Writer Anne Charters sees jazz as central to Kerouac's work:

> Spontaneous prose, in Kerouac's definition, takes on the semblance of linguistic entities unaligned with the conventional subject-verb arrangement of English sentences, thereby opening up the sense of time and allowing the movement, flashes, and fluctuations of jazz, and by extension, spiritual transcendence. (Charters in Kerouac, 2007: 9)

We've mentioned John Szarkowski already. In his perceptive descriptions of *The Americans*, he noticed something important: 'There was something almost casual, almost offhand, a little kind of syncopated carelessness, a kind of foot dragging rhythm to it.' (Livingston 1992: 308) Szarkowski is describing Frank's work as a 'Beat' document, and uses imagery stolen from music and particularly associated with jazz to describe it: 'casual', 'offhand', 'syncopated carelessness', 'foot dragging rhythm'. Jazz and wider musical ideas are important in *The Americans*, and offer some useful insights into its construction. As several of their friends noted, Frank and Kerouac were kindred spirits and their exploration of jazz aesthetics in their chosen forms is a key aspect of that kinship. *Time Magazine* in 1954 recorded that jazz musician Dave Brubeck 'thinks that modern jazz reflects the American scene' (Wall 2009). Given that Frank's quest was to record that scene, it is not surprising that several aspects of the practice of jazz are reflected in his work.

Jazz musicians often play a melody, frequently a very simple one, in a straightforward way at the beginning of a piece (this is usually called a 'head'). They then follow this with a series of solos, in which the ensemble improvises and plays around with the theme. This is a useful model for Frank's practice of exploring variations of particular visual leitmotifs. *The Americans* will often state a theme, then play with variations of it as it moves on, introducing new photographs as modifiers that deepen, expand and sophisticate the consideration. The car and the flag are good examples of 'heads', and will be considered in detail below.

Jazz, in part, grew out of and deconstructed classical forms. Charlie Parker's painstaking analysis of European *avant garde* scores is legendary. 'Classical' music is also often based around the establishment and development of themes. 'Sonata' form, for example, introduces a number of themes, which are then examined, developed and recapitulated. Jazz musicians were no less serious or intense, and sought to push back

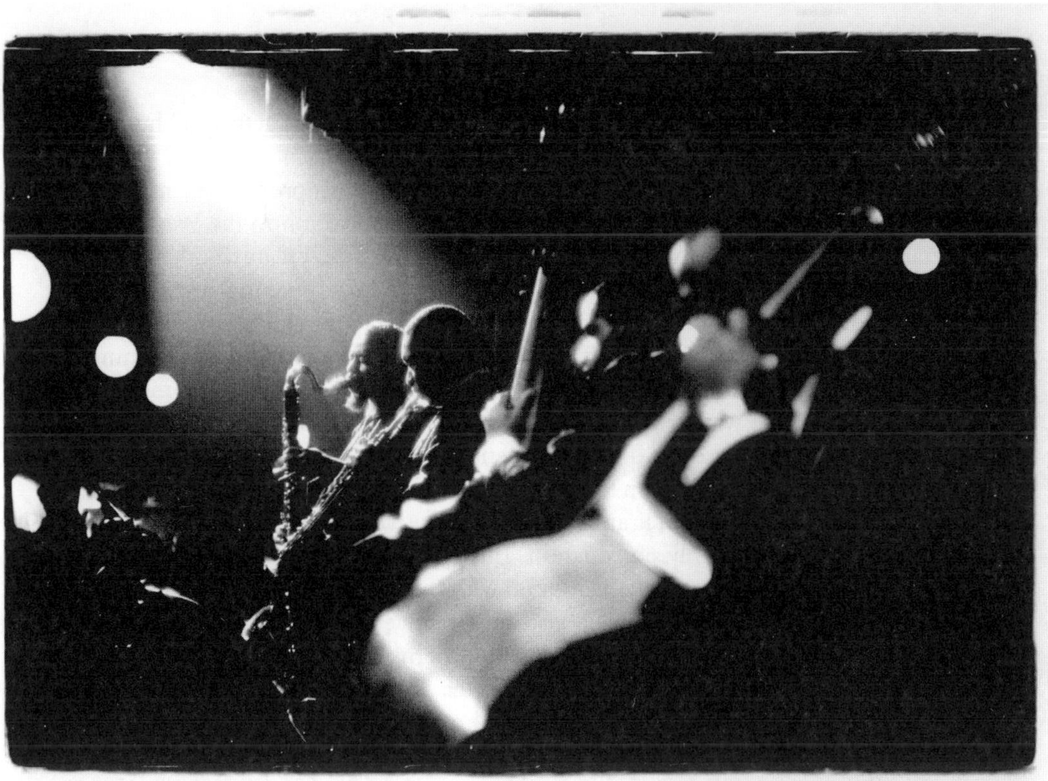

John Coltrane and Eric Dolphy, New York City, 1961 (Herb Snitzer/ Michael Ochs Archives/ Getty Images)

musical boundaries and explore new territory. As John Corbett wrote in *Jazz Amongst the Discourses,* it always sought to avoid the 'defiled and disfigured codes' (1995: 224). Frank had a similar intention: he consciously wanted to move away from accepted practice and innovate:

> I hate all those stories with a beginning, a middle and an end ... obviously I will make an effort to produce something that will stand up to all those stories but not be like them. (Frank, in Johnson 1989: 38)

Jazz pianist Dave Brubeck described his approach to composition as 'the search for something new within old forms, an unexpected perspective, a surprising order, an inner balance' (Wall 2009). This could be a description of Frank's approach to structure. The 'search for something new within old forms' is also evident. *The Americans* references and reworks several well-known paintings and etchings from the European visual canon. The contemporary idiom in which Frank re-presents these works disguises his sources so effectively that they have rarely been recognized or identified. Kerouac also felt this desire for new territory, the desire to transgress. He wrote: 'Man, wow there's so many things to do, so many things to write. How to get it down without getting all hung up on like literary inhibitions and grammatical fears.' (Kerouac 1972: 7)

'Improvisation' is another central aspect of jazz music. Improvisation may also be usefully called 'instantaneous composition'. Musical composition in the West is usually associated with studied and extended effort, a process which can create wonders, certainly, but which is at odds with the joyous spontaneity of music-making in the moment. Improvisation is the momentary, intuitive musical reaction to harmonic, melodic, emotional and cognitive shifts, playing off what has gone before and determining and constructing what will follow after. We've established that there is nothing 'momentary' about the painstaking way in which Frank selected the images for *The Americans*. His sequencing, however, was done quickly (Greenough 2009: 134).

Here is the seat and justification for Szarkowski's comments. Although I don't really see 'carelessness', the description of Frank's rapid and intuitive sequencing as 'foot dragging' is apposite and there is certainly syncopation. This musical notion describes the shifting of emphasis in musical rhythm, playing around with the beat, creating a shifting, changing pulse. It is characteristic of jazz. This is also an attractive description of the way in which Frank approaches his sequencing. He said, talking of his work in 1967: 'I wanted to create some kind of rhythm.' (Frank, in Greenough 2009: 177) Jazz players are often described as having a 'language'. This 'language' emerges through improvisation, during which it is honed, developed and polished over time. This idea of the 'polished improvisation' is an attractive description of the avowedly non-linear structuring of *The Americans*. Kerouac, again, did something similar in his writing:

> To achieve the improvisational creativity of the great jazz players, Kerouac experimented for several years before arriving at what Allen Ginsberg, referring to Kerouac's poetic sensibility, termed a 'modality of consciousness', signifying the aesthetic recreation of jazz improvisation in the creative prose of *On the Road.* (Charters, in Kerouac 2007: 9)

Both Kerouac and Frank were attracted by the thought of living in the moment, which is at the heart of improvisation. William Johnson has observed that Frank, more than anyone he has ever met, seeks to live in the present (1989: 28).

Frank's voluminous photographs, then, were taken as he travelled around America, encountering places, people and events in a thematically random manner, never neatly according to subject. The programming of *The Americans*, in its complexity, reflects the reality of Frank's journey and experience, and the mores of the milieu in which he moved. It is certain that Frank's departure from conventional narrative styles is so complete that many have mistaken his intentions completely.

Notes

1. The full text is:

> 'We work in unison with movement as though it were a presentiment of the way in which life itself unfolds. But inside movement there is one moment at which the elements in motion are in balance. Photography must seize upon this moment and hold immobile the equilibrium of it. A photographer composes a picture in very nearly the time it takes to click the shutter, at the speed of reflex action. Sometimes it happens that you stall, delay, wait for something to happen. Sometimes you have the feeling that here are all the makings of a picture—except for just one thing that seems to be missing. But what one thing? Perhaps someone walks into your range of view. You wait and wait and then finally you press the button—and you depart with the feeling (though you don't know why) that you've really got something. Later you can take a print and trace on it the geometric figures which come up and you'll observe that you have instinctively fixed a geometric pattern without which the photograph would have been both formless and lifeless. Composition must be one of our constant preoccupations, but at the moment of shooting it can stem only from our intuition for we are out to capture the fugitive moment and all the interrelationships are on the move.' (Cartier-Bresson 1952: 50)

2. Frank's working method relates interestingly to the process described by Roy Stryker, who ran both the Farm Security Administration and later the Standard Oil Picture File. A Picture File memo reveals his thinking. It suggests that proofs should be: 'cut up, organized and edited before caption writing begins. Taking the pictures in your hands, arranging them to see what kind of story they tell, is the only way to do good captioning and editing.' (Anonymous in Keller 1986: 37) There is no evidence that Frank was aware of Stryker's ideas, but he certainly knew his photographers. Walker Evans worked with Stryker at the government-funded Farm Security Administration, and it is possible that Frank came into contact with the latter's thoughts at second hand. Stryker is suggesting that photographs should be sequenced according to their inner character and relationships. He recognizes that a variety of relationships, and thereby a variety of meanings, may be achieved by a particular structuring of a series of photographs.

   We have noted already that images in *The Americans* are linked both thematically and visually. This, too, implies a kind of narrative intention. Stryker, interestingly, had discussed the possibility of a wordless photographic narrative in 1946: 'Your pictures are words of a peculiar sort. If they were words, remember that when you write you need nouns, verbs to give action, and above all modifiers.' (Stryker 1946: 49) Frank's photographs in *The Americans* function in this way, with a photograph establishing a theme, a discussion being initiated by a second, which is then sustained by a number of others before its conclusion is celebrated in a number of modifications. The images talk to each other. Being wordless, save for their captions, they speak to us in our own language: the words they stimulate are our own words, spoken softly by ourselves, to ourselves. Stryker again usefully summarizes this approach in his instructional pamphlet and slide presentation, *The Use of Photographs*: 'Sometimes one picture can tell the story but more often several pictures can tell it better… The message in a photograph is often strengthened by subsidiary pictures…The same story is better told as the sum of many parts.' (Stryker, in Keller 1986: 49)

In the same piece, he describes the use of 'a picture supported by an opposite' and 'a picture supported by a complement', which is what Frank so frequently does.

3. This concern with novelty is at the heart of Modernism, constructed as it is on assumptions about the perfectibility of humanity and our 'march towards the stars', developed out of the writings of Georg Hegel and others. From our current postmodern position, concerned as we are with sustainability, developing out of our understanding of the cyclical and repetitive nature of our existence as a species, returning always and inevitably back to where we are and where we have always been, this appears hopelessly idealistic and naive.

4. The influence of these ideas has been taken towards its apogee more recently by David Carson and others, notably in the magazine *Ray Gun*. It has become almost the house style of postmodernism.

5

Image and Text

The American edition of Frank's book was published with a caption opposite each photograph, tersely describing and locating the photographs. The only extended prose in the work was an introduction by Jack Kerouac.

The relationship between image and text has always been a complex and highly charged one. The French psychoanalyst Jacques Lacan, for example equates language with violence: he wrote in *The Language of the Self* that 'violence is originatory within language' (1968: 49). I have argued elsewhere (Day 2008: 45 et seq.) for language as a matrix of meaning and obfuscation. Frank conceived *The Americans* as a series of images from its outset. He wrote that he wished to create 'a document, the visual impact of which will nullify explanation' (Frank, in Maloney 1958: 115). He sought to escape the tyranny of words. Walker Evans shared his conviction. In the original introduction to *The Americans*, which was rejected and used instead to accompany the publication of some of Frank's fellowship photographs in the *US Camera Annual* of 1958, he wrote, 'For the thousandth time, it must be said that pictures speak for themselves, wordlessly, visually, or they fail.' (Evans, in Maloney 1958: 90)

Frank did not achieve his goal easily. *Les Americaines*, published by Frank's friend Robert Delpire in 1958 in Paris, juxtaposed Frank's photographs with writings by a variety of authors, chosen by Alain Bosquet. This followed the orthodoxy of the time, which believed that images needed text. Edwin Rosskam, one of Roy Stryker's Standard Oil photographers, expounded this philosophy:

> I began to get the idea that photography, in the sense of Farm Security and for that matter Standard Oil, is a language and that words are another language. The two things are beautifully fitted to each other to say what

> each is most able to say. And in books the principle is followed in the sense that whatever would normally be description is a picture, and whatever is abstraction or concept is written. (Rosskam, in Plattner 1983: 6)

Frank described things in his images, certainly, but he signally did not need text for his discussion of the abstract or conceptual.

We have noted that Frank chose to use short captions, indicating that he does not entirely reject language in his communication. Many of these captions direct the viewer's interpretations very specifically, but they do not equate to the extended copy in *Les Americaines*. The Scalo edition of *The Americans*, first published in 1993, relegated even these captions to the back of the book, suggesting an ambivalence towards them on Frank's part.[1]

The only extended text in *The Americans*, as noted above, was an introduction by Jack Kerouac. The original plan was for Walker Evans to write the introduction. There is sense in this: Evans was another Guggenheim laureate and was, by Frank's own admission, his teacher (Johnson 1989). Evans was a proficient writer, but Frank felt it was 'all wrong' and too concerned with the past (Greenough 2009: 137). Frank was moving in circles which intersected with the linguistic iconoclasm of the emerging Beat writers.[2] Frank recalls:

> I met Jack Kerouac on a hot summer night at a party in New York City. We sat down on the sidewalk, I showed Jack the photographs for *The Americans*. He said 'Sure I can write something about these pictures'. (Frank 1989: before the chapter headed 'United States')

and:

> I had met Jack Kerouac at a party given for him by his friend Lucien Carr. He was sitting on the sidewalk, around 18th or 19th Street, and I came there with a French edition of the book and I showed it to him. He liked the photos, and I said that you should write something for it. It was pretty relaxed. But Kerouac wrote the introduction. (Frank, in Johnson 1989: 42)

Kerouac was an inspired choice. He had attended college, but as a football scholar. He was an intellectual, certainly: his erudition is evident, with wide and detailed knowledge of American literature and of Buddhist writing. He was also a hipster and a bum, comfortable riding on the back of trucks and flat cars and dating waitresses. He had lived for many years in this way, a condition he had celebrated in his novel *Dharma Bums*, elevating the status of the vagabond and hobo to that of holy quester, equating the American tramp with the Saddhus of India and the wandering monks of East Asia. It may be argued that many Old

World artists shared these traits. A good number were equally interested in contemporary ideas and fashion, equally as poor and equally as interested in waitresses as Kerouac. Perhaps Picasso is as good an example as we need. The difference lies Kerouac's sense of mission and of self. There is no apparent association in his mind between the notion of 'artist' or 'writer' and the elitism that was (and to a large degree still is) at the heart of European culture. He was not 'slumming it' as an artist, not wallowing in underclass life socially while associating with the rich and famous in galleries. He was fully part of the world of his characters, not an aloof observer but an equal-status participant. Significantly, his ancestry was part First American, further rooting him on American soil and in American history. All of these 'credentials' emphasized Kerouac as a child of the New World, and underlie the exciting new approach to creativity developed by the Beats, born of that world and in marked contrast to so much of the 'high' art mindset of the Old one. Kerouac's is a literature of the streets, not pulp fiction by any means, but accessible and relevant to a wide demographic.

Kerouac, furthermore, shared Frank's concern regarding the strait-jacketing of creativity by traditional practices. In some ways he was an expressionist writer capturing the world as he saw it, quickly in words on paper, according to his own lights and in his own 'colours'. He was famously reticent to change anything once it was in black and white, believing the first draft to be in some mystical sense 'holy' (Kerouac 1992: 57).

Kerouac's writing evidences his desire for 'direct' experience as it is described in Zen writings. He sought to live and see in a way unaltered by the goggles and filters that are forced on to us by our socialization. His quest became ever more urgent as the foundational assumptions of their society were revealed as questionable and compromised. This desire for directness is central to the Buddhist writings so beloved of Kerouac, particularly writings in the Zen tradition (Various 2009). This desire for directness also plays its part in Kerouac's approach to communication, absorbing his experiences and then expressionistically recalling and recording them, describing and understanding what has passed, according to his vision.

Kerouac's approach is a clear analogue, in text, to Frank's photography. They are both striving to see beyond the externally imposed 'dream' of America, those aspects which in Buddhism are called *Samsara*: the world of illusions. Frank's photograph *Fourth of July, Jay New York* wonderfully evidences this. It reveals America in its all its banality, beside and beneath its tattered and repaired flag. Simultaneously, it contrasts this with an evanescent and ethereal vision of trees and sky, seen through the fabric of its Stars and Stripes (see *People of the Flag* below for further consideration of this image).

Despite their commonality, there are significant differences in Frank's and Kerouac's approaches. The 'syncopation' and 'foot dragging rhythm' within the photographs, and the speed with which they were sequenced, are close to Kerouac's work. We have noted already that Frank's painstaking selection of images, over a period of four or so months (Greenough 2009: 137), makes *The Americans* a finely considered document, carefully thought over and determined, which is in contrast to the three weeks in which Kerouac famously wrote *On the Road* (1957). Nevertheless, in his 'Beat' approach and in the stylistic experiments he undertook, Kerouac was as near as a writer could be to sharing Frank's aims.

Frank paid a price for his insistence on the primacy of a visual mode of communication. Many readers struggle to see any meaning in his work. Jefferson Hunter says: 'in *The Americans* he (Frank) does without an editorializing or commenting text of any kind.' He calls Frank 'a specialist in the sense of stripping his photographs of any possible social or political meaning' (1987: 50). Implicit in this analysis is an association between a lack of text and lack of meaning. Hunter suggests that without words there can be no analysis, comment or intention on the part of the photographer. Without the familiar directed reading of a photograph provided by text, he is unable to penetrate Frank's wordless work. This would be impossible with Steichen's clearly annotated *The Family of Man* (1955).

The French critic and art historian Jean Clay, talking about painting, describes the notion of the 'submission' of images to words, as it was propounded by Rosskam, Stryker and other contemporaries of Frank:

> In the face of this arbitrariness of the linguistic pattern, the submission of painting (to language) is seen in two ways. On the one hand, the figure has no material existence: its only value is that of an image concept, and it finds its legitimacy only in its relationship to what it refers. On the other hand everything in the painting that is not figurative is considered worthless. The only thing that counts is what can be named. (Clay 1978: 14)

The image, essentially, is seen as description, illustrating ideas expressed elsewhere.

These ideas are associated with the notion of 'semiotics', which was developed in the writings of Ferdinand De Saussure (1995) and others, which were well established and extensively explored by the 1950s. The notion of images operating as 'word equivalents', with intrinsic semantics and grammar, was widely accepted. Frank's *Covered car – Long Beach, California* is a fine example. The photograph depicts a car covered in a cloth. The cloth appears to be silk, perhaps a parachute or something similar. The richly adorned car stands between two palm trees, which create the impression of a portico. The car thus becomes an altar, complete with altar cloth. In case this notion might appear overly fanciful, the book's next image supports and confirms it. *Car accident – US 66, between Winslow and Flagstaff, Arizona* pictures corpses hidden beneath a tarpaulin. These are the sacrifices consequent on the culture of the car. The silk-covered automobile, the palm trees and the house at the photograph's rear are all 'words' in the photograph's 'story'. There is even an implicit grammar. We 'read' the car in the foreground before we do the trees and the house, suggesting, as I am sure Frank intended, that it is the subject of the sentence, more important than the trees or house, which merely modify and deepen its meaning.

Frank, then, does not need words to explain his photographs; they are themselves eloquent. As Walker Evans argues, 'Pictures speak for themselves or they fail' (in Maloney 1958: 90). There is more, though. Picasso said 'It's useless to paint what it's possible to describe' (to J. Metzinger 1910 in Clay 1978: 15). In other words, sophisticated images ideally need to transcend the notions of 'word equivalency' and 'visual language' taken from semiotics. Jean Clay writes:

> This subordination (of image) to language goes so far that the artist in his observation of the outer world sees only what he can delineate, outline, quantify. Nature is a nomenclature. The rest participates in the 'unmentionable'—and therefore in the unfigurable. Beginning with Cezanne, modern art devoted itself to summoning this 'unmentionable'. (Clay 1978: 14)

This is vital for Frank. From the mid-nineteenth century, Western art was trying to escape the 'tyranny' of language, as theorized in semiotics, in an attempt to free perception from the heavy-handed direction of nomenclature. The painter Paul Cezanne, working in the late nineteenth century, had begun to abandon the traditional differentiation between highly worked, significant foreground objects and the background, which simply served to contain them. He questioned the notion of visual hierarchy and gave equal attention to foreground and background. He began to integrate these in works like *Fruit bowl with glass and apples* (1879–82, location unknown) or *Mont Sainte Victoire seen from Les Lauves* (1902, Philadelphia Museum of Art). The Cubists took this further in their destruction of the separated integrity of objects. Painter George Braque's *The Portuguese* (1911, Kunstmuseum, Basle) or Delaunay's *The Eiffel Tower with Trees* (1909, Guggenheim Museum, New York) exemplify the interpenetration of what were previously distinct objects and ground. This breakdown of boundaries facilitated a discussion in these works of those things that are not easily depicted, that exist behind or between objects—'time' and 'energy' are examples. These are mercurial forces which cannot be directly seen, and whose presence must be intimated through their effects, visible all around. Figuring them is as difficult as seeing them, and must be accomplished in an analogous manner.

Frank often sought nothing so resolutely as to photograph the indescribable, 'the essence of the black and white, of where God is' (Frank 1991: after plate 63). A beautiful example is *Crosses on scene of highway accident – US 91, Idaho.* Frank photographed a road flanked by three simple white crosses, an image that could be read as simply a memorial to three road accident victims. It is followed by *Assembly line Detroit,* a car factory staffed by oily, busy line workers. This later can be seen as a comment on the means of the victims' destruction. Men make cars, which then destroy men. If this were an adequate analysis of Frank's work, then a simple 'word equivalent' reading would suffice. It is not. Streaming from the top of *Crosses on scene of highway accident* is a flare of light. It recalls an austere, ascetic rendering of a Renaissance image of heaven and earth, the host of heaven hovering above the material plane. Even more closely, it recalls Rembrandt's celebrated *Three Crosses* engraving (1653, Rijksmuseum, Amsterdam), as we will see later. The shaft of white light above the markers contrasts sharply with the dirty greys of the factory opposite, giving the latter an almost infernal suggestion. Frank conjures heaven and hell in the almost invisible space between his pictures. He discusses the possibility of the release death brings from the earthly drudgery signified by the factory, a return to the divine. As St Paul said in Corinthians, 'now we see through a glass darkly; but then face to face!' (Various 1958: 170).

Frank sought to picture both the material and the immaterial through the quality of his images' moments and their interrelation.

We noted that Pablo Picasso said 'It's useless to paint what it's possible to describe'. This figure, who was so hugely influential in the art scene in New York in the 1950s, is effectively describing Frank's faith in the power of the image.

Paul Valery said 'poetry is the space between word and meaning' (Valery, in Clay 1978: 15). Between the physical materiality of its compositions and that of which they speak lies the poetry of *The Americans.*

Notes

1. Significantly, much of Frank's later work features text inscribed into photographs, which further attests to his exploitation of language. *Sick of Goodbyes* (1978, National Gallery of Art) and *Pablo* (1979, National Gallery of Art) are examples.

2. An example of Frank's social involvement with 'Beat' society, albeit after *The Americans,* is provided by Sue Mingus, the wife of bass player and composer Charles Mingus:

    > I met Mingus at the Five Spot. At the time I had a brief film career. I was in a film by Robert Frank, he's one of our great photographers, known for a book called *The Americans* about the Beats and the late 50s, he also directed *Pull my Daisy* with Allen Ginsberg. I was in one of his films and we were looking for Ornette Coleman to do a soundtrack, and I was going around to jazz clubs with Robert and our producer. I knew nothing about jazz at all and I met Mingus while he was performing at the Five Spot. (Mingus 1997: n.p.)

3. It should be noted that Carol Cassady, Kerouac's sometime lover and wife of his friend Neal, comments that what Kerouac says about writing prose and what he actually did were not the same thing (Cassady 2007).

Part Two

Themes in *The Americans*

Having examined the conditions which prevailed at the time, and the particular set of experiences and predilections that led Frank to create the Americans, it is finally time to dive into the fecund and absorbing world which is held within his photographs.

Perhaps the most immediate impression made by *The Americans* is the sense of arcane linkages between often quite widely separated images. The car is perhaps the most obvious example, occurring here and there throughout most of the book, in photographs that seem to have something to say about this mechanical creation and its owners and pilots. The flag, similarly, is scattered throughout the book commenting, it seems, in a profound if not immediately obvious way on this powerful symbol. These over-arching 'themes' are a major architectural feature of the book, and the photographs that carry them warrant consideration together first. These photographs state, comment on, modify and resolve thematic considerations, and are structured intuitively in the ways that we have examined above.

Part Three will look at the sequential linkages that exist within *The Americans*. These are complementary to the thematic connections, and a full picture of Frank's work can only emerge from an appreciation of both views. We will see that it is possible to determine links between adjacent pairs of images, both visually and thematically, links which create triptychs and quadtychs, and links which exist between extended sequences of images. These allow the examination and discussion of several ideas and notions within the same photograph, and it is important to keep this in mind as we begin our thematic consideration. Perhaps the greatest injustice Frank and *The Americans* have suffered is the neglect of the deeply playful aspects of the work. This neglect may have resulted from a lack of balance between analysis of the non-sequential, thematically linked images and the linear sequences.

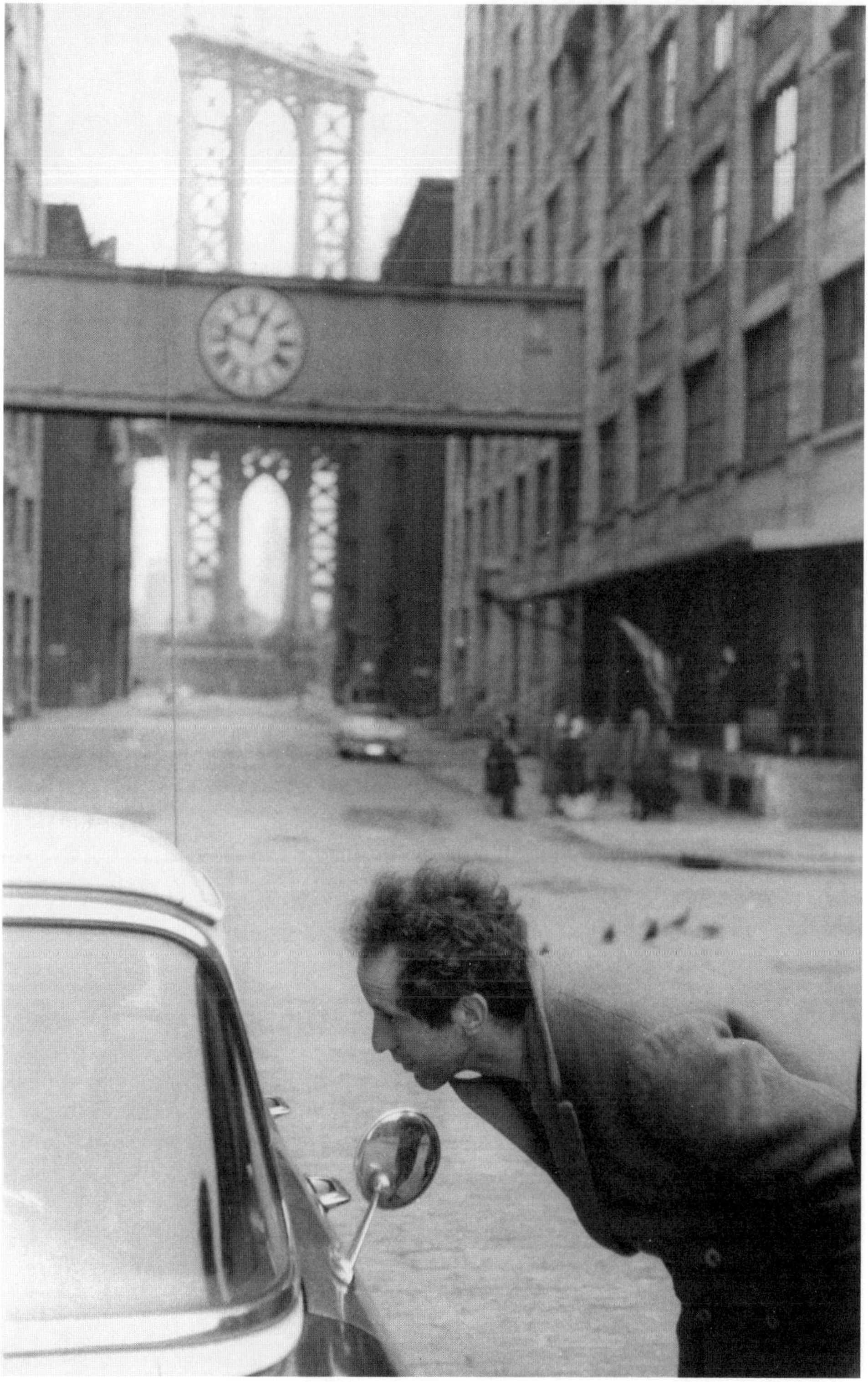

Robert Frank looking towards the Manhattan Bridge in the Brooklyn nighbourhood, during the shooting of a scene for a film, New York, 01 Jan 1957. (Photo by John Cohen/Getty Images)

6

People of the Flag

The American flag is its country's most recognizable symbol. It is a pictogram of nationhood, of unity, of the American way. In songs and dreams, it flies from a high White House or is raised by passionate Marine hands on Iwo Jima. Frank, not surprisingly, chose to structure *The Americans* around this strongest of ciphers. His initial *maquette* was arranged in four sections, each divided by a blank page and introduced by a flag (Greenough 2009: 133). The dividing pages were removed in the final editions, aiding the book's continuity. Flags nonetheless remain highly significant within the work, and are crucial to its intent.

Parade – Hoboken, New Jersey is the book's opening photograph. Two women stand in separate windows in a wall. On the left, a fat lady in a spotted dress stares grimly out. Next to her is another in a clean, buttoned coat, her face hidden by the flag's flap. The caption tells us why the flag is tied to the window: there is a parade.

Alfred Eisenstaedt provides a telling contrast in his iconic *V-J Day in Times Square* (1945, *Life* archives, Getty Museum). This photograph is principally a celebration of spontaneous human joy, but it is also a celebration of Americans and America. The dark-uniformed sailor kisses a young nurse, whose glorious transient beauty is defined in an exposed stocking top. Frank's women, by contrast, are faceless and grimacing. Eisenstaedt's revellers celebrate a Brave New World, a world at peace, a world which had just capitulated, through conflict, to the Anglo-American way. Whatever reason Frank's heroine had for tying a flag to her window, appears, from her expression, to have little to do with goodwill to all men. Frank reveals, as his frontispiece, a misanthropic stare at the heart of the parade. This photograph, in turn, is the heart of *The Americans*. Frank invites his readers to look at the American flag waving in its everyday reality, away from the hype and the lionizing. His photograph questions and modifies the received wisdom created by so many images of smiling flag-wavers. He said in his Statement in the 1958 *US Camera Annual*, 'It is important to see what is invisible to others perhaps the look of hope or the look of sadness.' (Frank, in Maloney 1958: 115). He is looking to photograph that which is occluded, those moments that might be caught in the corner of an eye and dismissed. The critic and galleryist Jane Livingston recognized that Frank captured 'things found around the edges, things half invisible to most of us most of the time' (1992: 343).

This askance seeing, deliberately avoiding the orthodoxies of enculturation, is not the only challenge of *Parade – Hoboken*. A brick wall occupies the centre of the picture. It is blandly regular, jerry-built, functional without beauty. Its dominance of the photograph challenges viewers' expectations. Images that include human beings very often make them the principal subject. Here they are marginalized, cramped into the corners of the composition. They appear no more important in the image's visual hierarchy than the wall which divides them.[1] These women are fitted into this block not because it suits them or is a desirable residence, but because there is nowhere else they can go. The photograph's tenement claustrophobia is heightened by the cropped flag and window frames, and by the almost unbearably close picture plane. Frank has achieved a foreshortening through his head-on view. All of the objects in the photograph are at about the same distance from the camera. This unrelenting flatness invades our personal space; it is too close for comfort. The photograph's viewpoint is at the level of the women's rooms, implying another window across the street. The horizon of their vision is, then, defined by another brick wall.[2]

This photograph is about alienation. The women are divided by their wall from each other within the house and divided from the parade below. The house separates them and, even more surely, keeps them from us. The claustrophobic picture plane is an effective stylistic analogue to their tenement reality. There is no association here between the flag and beautiful, youthful exuberance, no admirable sentiments, no smiling face or stocking tops. There is ugliness, banality and a tantalizing glimpse of Frank's dense and challenging intention.

Frank talked of his work in terms of 'love' (in Maloney 1958: 115) and 'vision' (1954 in Tucker and Brookman 1986: 20), so there must be more to *Parade – Hoboken* if he is not to be proved a liar. These women are not demons, they are everyday. They have to live in this forbidding place, but something in their thrown-up, four-square lives must surely embody their hope, if they are to survive. Karl Marx, talking about the religious inclination in humanity, wrote: 'Religion is the sigh of the oppressed creature, the heart of a heartless world, and the soul of soulless conditions.' (Marx 1977: 127) However fatuous or compromised, the Stars and Stripes is the nearest thing the women have to a symbol for their wild hope, a conduit for their doubting and uncertain faith. In the back-street reality of the American Dream, real women still take a moment out of their lives to stand beside it and watch a parade.

The ugliness of *Parade – Hoboken* was too much for many of Frank's readers. Bruce Downs, writing in *Popular Photography* in 1960, commented:

> Frank is sensitive, but apparently he is without love. There is no pity in his images. They are images of hate and hopelessness, of desolation and preoccupation with death. They are images of America by a man who hates the country of his adoption … It is a world shrouded in immense grey tragic boredom. (Downs, in Tucker and Brookman 1986: 36)

John Durniak wrote in the same publication, 'If this is America (the United States) we should burn it down and start again' (in Tucker and Brookman 1986: 36). James Zanutto, paraphrasing Kerouac, called it a 'sad poem for sick people' (in Tucker and Brookman 1986: 37). Even with the benefit of hindsight, there is something in these criticisms that carries a disturbing kernel of truth. How do we square the undoubted ugliness and desperate disempowerment of Frank's Hoboken women? Perhaps Marx again says it best:

> To call on them (humanity) to give up their illusions about their condition is to call on them to give up a condition that requires illusions. The criticism of religion is, therefore, in embryo, the criticism of that vale of tears of which religion is the halo. (Marx 1977: 127)

As long as people suffer, they will need dreams. Surely *Parade – Hoboken* is Frank's 'criticism coming out of love'. He is facing and describing this 'grey tragic boredom' in the hope of contributing towards bringing it to an end. We have noted already that Frank wrote: 'I think at that time I was compassionate. I had a feeling of compassion for the people on the street.' (Frank, in Wheeler 1977: 22).

At the same time as allowing the idly flapping flag to simultaneously embody and challenge hope, Frank presses it further into a manifesto for his book. A woman's face, the thing that most characterizes human beings as individuals, is here obscured by the flag. *The Americans* is an examination of the nature of a people, a look through a flag at the faces hidden behind it, and the extent to which these faces are stained by its red, white and blue.[3]

In a typically Frank action, always defeating expectations in order to stimulate engagement, the next flag picture included has no association with a chapter heading function. *Navy Recruiting Station, Post Office – Butte, Montana* features the flag as one among many motifs. It hangs vertically in an office lit by daylight. Set against a dark framing door, the Star Spangled Banner supplies the entry point into this photograph. It points down at the recruiting officer's indolently crossed feet. These rest on his desk, over a sign saying 'Join the Navy, ask me about it.' The ironic juxtaposition of the conventional dream of the dynamic glory of the US Navy with the tawdry, typically small-town, somnolent office is supported by the flag, but does not rely on it, perhaps accounting for this slight anomaly.

The Americans' second 'section-introducing' flag photograph is *Fourth of July – Jay, New York*. A huge Stars and Stripes hangs above a lawn. The composition looks casual, rather snapshot. A bored young boy walks out of the bottom left corner of the photograph, his legs and arm cropped. Opposite him, in the bottom right corner, a man in shirtsleeves is also cropped. He chats to another man. Behind the flag, people amble around. Two girls in white party dresses, balloons in hand, run towards it. Theirs is the only focused activity in the photograph.

This is the Fourth of July, Independence Day, a day on which America celebrates itself. It remembers the break with European hypocrisy, class divisions and tyranny, and represents the dream of a new way, a new and better life. The flag is the symbol of all this, yet here it hangs torn, mended and mostly ignored. Its reality as a piece of faded, damaged cloth is clearly displayed. The symbol is thus subverted by its own materiality. The flag's patchwork questions America's shiny chrome dream. The flawless future of this flawless state is revealed as a much-used and repaired conception, more rustic than utopian, brought out by a stolid populus as they celebrate their unremarkable holiday. The Dream represented by the flag cannot be too pressing or imminent, since no one in the photograph pays it any attention. They are concerned, instead, with their families, their neighbours and themselves. Everyday America is again emphatically revealed.

We discussed this interest in the vernacular and everyday earlier, considering the growing focus on the lives and actions of the ordinary working people as an understandable reaction to the bankruptcy of European culture, with its aristocratic, hierarchical power structures. It is also evidenced, wonderfully, by the painter Jasper Johns in his *Flag* of 1954 (Museum of Modern Art, New York). Johns' work used the archaic technique of encaustic, along with paint. Melted wax is used to build a textured surface. Beneath the wax, Johns placed cut out newspaper fragments, echoing the earlier Cubist collages of Picasso and others. Just as the copy on the newspaper fragments was sometimes part of the Cubists' intent, so it is important in Johns' piece. His clippings come from the small advertisements and anecdotal stories on the back pages of small-town American journals. He creates the icon of American identity from the humble happenings and concerns of its everyday unexceptional people. This is clearly a concern and a predilection powerfully shared by Frank.

Much of the landscape in *Fourth of July – Jay, New York* is seen through the flag. As with *Parade – Hoboken*, Frank photographs the flag as a filter through which its country is perceived. The trees and grass of its reality, like its people, are seen through the constructs of its red, white and blue. America sees itself, and is seen, through its dream. These preconceptions are almost impossible to ignore. Frank wanted to examine the reality within and behind the flag, within and behind America's public face, and invites us to join him in the exploration.

Bar – Detroit initiates the third 'section'. This photograph records the upper part of a bar's wall and some of its ceiling. Central to the image is an illuminated American flag, caught between darkly toned portraits of George Washington to the left and Abraham

Lincoln to the right. A plaster cornice delineates the ceiling, and faux half-timbering covers the wall beneath the trio of portraits and flag. These architectural details provide a rooting in the everyday world for these airy symbols. The framed portraits embody an older world, one of formality and even decorum. They speak of a serious world, in which appropriate gravitas is reserved and required for these American founding fathers and inspirational leaders. This gravitas contrasts markedly with the illuminated flag. It is difficult to be certain of the materials of its manufacture, but it appears to be vacuum-moulded plastic, lit from within by a bulb. An industrially mass-produced rendition, then, of the Stars and Stripes. This contrasts markedly with the hand-restored and maintained flag of *Jay, New Jersey*. Furthermore the moulded flag appears to be slowly collapsing, wilting under its own weight and peeling away from the wall. This juxtaposition of presentational modes is powerful and reveals the iconoclasm wrapped up in the industrial consumerist explosion. The old forms, with all their seriousness and immanent value, are ranged alongside the cheap, ephemeral and industrial; both expressions seen as equally appropriate carriers of American identity.

Beneath this trio, a sign saying 'You must be 21 and prove' hangs near to a cartoon-like carving of a fish. Frank is celebrating the facility of the vernacular decorators who created this assemblage. The grandly patriotic, the pragmatic and the utterly kitsch are combined without self-consciousness. These icons are given equality by their proximity. These Americans happily hang long-dead presidents next to something more akin to Mickey Mouse. It is not seen as inappropriate. America exists within both these visual strophes, and within their relationship to each other. Both are essential to an understanding of this civilization.

Much of the joy of *The Americans* lies in its visual playfulness. I am very attracted to a final possibility within the image. The ceiling of the bar is spangled with spots of light. It is difficult to see how this has been achieved, whether there is reflective material included in the stuff from which it is made or whether some glittering light-source is responsible, but these glowing dots cover its expanse. They fall into the waffle-like pattern on the ceiling's plaster. All of this is reflected in the glass of Lincoln's portrait. The rectilinear pattern and the shiny dots conspire to produce an accidental stars and stripes, not preconceived or intentional, draped around the president like a stole or the *aegis* of a Greek god. Next to a plastic realization of the real thing, an architectural accident drapes the president in a self-emanated celebration of nationhood. Manifest destiny in Detroit. I can almost see the ironic smile on Frank's face.

Political rally – Chicago, the final section-initiating image, is witty and in many ways a joke. Its depiction of a Sousaphone-playing bandsman is playful, and echoes Cartier Bresson's wit and *bonhomie*. This is Frank, though, so of course the image functions in other ways too. As with the woman at the beginning of the book, in the window in *Parade – Hoboken*, the bandsman is rendered headless, this time by his instrument. His body is a compound of flesh, uniform and metal tubing, creating an image of a composite being, whose clear purpose is to act as a mouthpiece. We are shown what this mouthpiece is for by the flags which appear to stream out of the horn of the instrument, festooning the building with stars and stripes. The instrument itself speaks so powerfully of America, invented as it was by an emigré musician who combined an aspect of his name 'So', with 'USA' in order to create himself anew in this new world. The performer here sports a badge, 'Adlai'. There are two images in *The Americans* entitled *Political Rally – Chicago.* This repetition is inviting us to consider this image alongside the much earlier portrait of an effusive, suited man, declaiming his faith in something or other from a ledge. The building stone in both images is similar, and it may well be that the members of this band are the suited man's heralds, sonorously supporting his rhetoric from below. The implication, of course, is the loss of self. The bandsman's individuality and self-determination are sacrificed, along with his head and face, such powerful signifiers of selfhood, to his vocation. What price the work of a mouthpiece?

We've noted that this final flag image replicates and comments on the book's first, *Parade – Hoboken.* Both are decapitations, and they bracket the book's consideration of this most powerful symbol of nationhood. Although the circumstances and the complicity of the participants in these images are very different, both photographs evidence the stripes of red, white and blue that America indelibly paints across its inhabitants. While one is uncertain and tentative, perhaps even a victim, nervously holding her hand to her mouth, as if to quiet her doubts and fears, her 'yes, buts …' as the celebratory parade passes, the other is a feet-first adherent, gladly taking his role of uniform and herald.

In his exploitation of the flag as introduction and punctuation, Frank states his intention for *The Americans.* He wrote to his parents, 'I am working hard not just to photograph, but to give an opinion in my photos of America' (Frank, in Tucker and Brookman 1986: 28). His opinion is expressed in his celebration and deconstruction of the flag. Frank's photographs catch the flag with its guard down. They depict it outside of its conventional settings, in situations without beauty or heroism. By this shifting of context, Frank questions and reveals the processes by which the Star Spangled Banner's meaning was constructed. He tears it away from the White House and Iwo Jima, and shows its reality in Hoboken or Jay. Frank tests the symbol, in order to understand the civilization for which it stands.

His conclusion is ambivalent. The Sousaphone player is subsumed by the Stars and Stripes, his identity destroyed, while the flag in Hoboken, for all the uncertainty of its flyers, may be all they have of colour and joy. It is the nearest thing to hope in that desolation. The people of Jay trot out their much-repaired ensign and ignore it. It doesn't dominate them. In Detroit, the flag is merely one symbol among many, pressed into service by the owners and drinkers in a bar. It satisfies their needs. If the red, white and blue consumes some of its people, other Americans take it and mould it into their own likeness.

Notes

1. This marginalization and use of people as minor compositional elements had been used before, but not perhaps as radically as in this photograph. Jacob Riis, in *Under the Dump*, records a collection of refuse beneath a wooden structure. Amongst the rags, boxes and bags is a rather inconspicuous bent figure. The visual dominance of the central supporting beam and the beautifully captured chiaroscuro leave this little man as a seeming afterthought. He is, at best, an aspect of the dump. This is emphasized by Riis's title. A portrait usually mentions its subject. *Under the Dump* reveals this vagrant as an element in the landscape, ironically emphasizing Riis's humanist message. Frank's caption follows suit.

2. Interestingly, this echoes much of photographer Timothy O'Sullivan's work. Frank has no foreground here, only a little empty air between the women's cell-like rooms and our viewpoint. Much of the work of the early American landscape photographers avoided any foreground. This implies a separation, the photograph as the visual, scientific report of the disinterested surveyor. It is possible to extend this argument to include Frank.

3. *Parade – Hoboken* relates in several ways to Cartier Bresson's *New England* of 1933 (collection of Magnum). This was included in *The Decisive Moment*, published in 1952. Here another woman, this time ancient, emaciated and arthritic, stands in front of a board house. She has a Stars and Stripes around her neck, presumably serving as an apron. Her withered appearance and the dirty yard in some ways resemble Frank's work. However, her expression is undefeated, suggesting that she has survived unbroken and won through her adversities. Perhaps the photograph implies that the dream of America, the dream of a better life tomorrow, embodied by the flag, has sustained her. She points off to the right in a gesture redolent of Michelangelo's Adam, pointing at God in the Sistine Chapel (c. 1511). This duality of perception, the implication of a wry smile on the photographer's lips, is classic Cartier-Bresson. Frank sees another equally valid aspect of America—one which encouraged fewer smiles.

4. The contact sheets show that these images are from the same time, the first being catalogued by Frank as 'Chicago 25' and the second as 'Chicago 18', both from 1956 (Greenough 2009: 376–77).

7

On the Road

Central to the impact and success of *The Americans* is Frank's recognition and presentation of significant symbols which act to define America's emerging civilization. These include filling stations, diners, jukeboxes and, perhaps most eloquently of all, the automobile. Frank images cars that are present at conception, that serve as nannies and childhood friends, cars that facilitate romance, are the seat of great endeavours and the objects of worship, cars that perpetrate murder and become the conduits and memorials of the dead. The notion of a life lived *On the Road* is not unique to Frank, reflecting, rather, an allegory of life's journey and the pursuit of paradise on earth widely expressed and examined in near-contemporary culture. Jack Kerouac's novel (1957), along with F. Scott Fitzgerald's *The Great Gatsby* (1925), films such as *Of Mice and Men* (Milestone 1939) and *The Grapes of Wrath* (Ford 1940), alongside *Rebel Without a Cause* (Ray 1955) and *The Wild One* (Benedek 1954) and experimental and innovative music from John Coltrane, Charlie Parker and Woody Guthrie all enfold Frank's series of pictures.

The road and car are highly significant in American culture. Frank himself chose a 1950 second-hand Ford Business Coupe and the road as the conduit for his Guggenheim Foundation funded study. It is not surprising that the highway should feature so prominently in *The Americans*. Kerouac's *On the Road* was finished in the same year as the publication in France of the first version of Frank's book, *Les Americaines* by Robert Delpire. Kerouac describes the call of the road for his generation:

> I wanted to take off. Somewhere along the line I knew there'd be girls, visions, everything. Somewhere along the line the pearl would be handed to me. I could see Denver looming ahead of me like the promised land, way out there beneath the stars, across the prairie of Iowa and the plains of Nebraska. (Kerouac 1972: 11)

Kerouac's exuberance sets him a little apart from Frank, but the notion of quest, seeking some kind of latter-day grail, is common to both artists. Frank described his goal for this journey as: 'lying in wait, pursuing, sometimes catching … the knowledge of where God is' (Frank 1991: after plate 63).

The still-new American interstate network and the wide, wild vastness of America were an appropriate place to look. There is an association between travelling these roads and the spiritual: they are an analogue for the journey we all undertake. *U.S. 285 New Mexico* shows the highway at its most open. Ruler straight, it bisects the semi-desert and the photograph. A tiny car in the middle distance is the only other object in the photograph. This heightens the smallness and impermanence of the traveller next to the monumentality of the road. Light reflects off the tarmac as far as the distant horizon. It bifurcates in the foreground, following the ruts left by tyres. The illuminated road cuts across the dark desert like a highway under some enchantment. It rises in the distance, appearing to point up into the sky. The overtones of a charmed path leading to a bright place, perhaps paradise, appear to be denied by the lowering sky. There is more. A thin band of light stands between the illusory apex of the road and the dark sky. The light appears almost to leak along the horizon, as if the shining road has punctured the darkness. Is this the promise of the end of the road, Kerouac's 'pearl' or Frank's 'knowledge of where God is'? It is literally the suggestion of enlightenment, if only the end may be reached. However uncertain the destination, the road to it is undeniably luminous. Whatever the journey's end may be, the travelling will be along its brightness, riding between darkness to the left and right.

This figuring of the road echoes Dorothy's journey along the Yellow Brick Road in the film *The Wizard of Oz* (Vidor et al. 1939) and F. Scott Fitzgerald, writing thirty years earlier, who said:

> Out of the corner of his eye Gatsby saw that the blocks of the sidewalks really formed a ladder and mounted to a secret place above the trees. He could climb to it, if he climbed alone, and once there he could suck on the pap of life, gulp down the incomparable milk of wonder. (Fitzgerald 1994: 118)

Gatsby, like Frank, Kerouac and Dorothy, dreams of paradise at the end of the road. Frank's engagement with this particular road is obvious. It dominates its environment. The entire lower three-quarters of the image is filled with tarmac. The camera angle shows Frank is on this bright road, photographing as he drives. Only the tiny, distant car speaks of others. This is the road less travelled. Frank described his experiences:

> 1955. I cross the States. For a year. 500 rolls of film. I go into post offices, Woolworths, 10 cent shops, bus stations. I sleep in cheap hotels. Around 7 in the morning I go to a nearby bar. I work all the time. I don't speak much. I try not to be seen. (Frank 1991: after plate 63)

A lonely journey by his own admission.

Frank had made images like this before, but they had included people. During his travels in 1948, he made *Peru* (R. Frank, 1948, collection of W. Zryd), which was included in *Indiens pas Morts*, published in 1956. This composition also has the road rising vertically towards the horizon, but the foreground is peopled by Peruvians in an assortment of bright tones and strange hats. The desert scrub is almost as bright as the dirt road, and a dramatic sky fills almost half of the image. Significantly, though, the viewpoint is from amongst his fellow travellers, precariously perched atop what we infer to be a vehicle of some sort.

Nearer is his *34th Street, New York, 1949*. The composition is very like *U.S. 285, New Mexico*, the road similarly occupying three-quarters of the photograph. The people depicted are far away and anonymous, insignificant next to the drama of the white striped, black macadamed street. New York's noise seems distant against the purity of monochrome, its chaotic bustle ugly against the purity of line. These images provide staging posts in Frank's record of his changing predilections; moving away from fellow travellers, setting out alone. The shared experience of Peru becomes the solitary personal journey of *U.S. 285*. This photograph's lack of street furniture, with its implication of community, leaves only the bare road as the most basic mark of civilization on the wilderness. This is a place of pilgrimage, an appropriate place for a journey of the spirit.

This view of the road was not universal. Walker Evans' *Frame Houses, Atlanta, Georgia* (1936, archive of the Farm Security Administration) passionately critiques it. Evans' photograph looks across a concrete highway at two frame houses. Although grubby and weatherbeaten, curtains in the houses' windows reveal that they are still occupied. The houses still retain at least a vestige of elegance. Ornate balconies and long, open front porches suggest a place for sitting in the evening and watching the world go by. This is no longer possible. The view is stopped by a wall and fence delineating the highway's edge. Perhaps this new road was once a dirt track, which served these houses. Now their prospect is unimportant next to the demands of the highway and its ever-increasing population. The original fence was penetrated by gates. Even these are now covered over by hoardings. Film posters advertise Anne Shirley in *Chatterbox*, and Carole Lombard, staring blonde and lascivious out of black-rimmed eyes, advertises *Love Before Breakfast*. The lives of real Americans have been pasted over by the ephemera of Hollywood. Their home, the place where they live out the reality of their lives, has been compromised and degraded in the cause of mass mobility.

The American Dream requires the notion of travel. If its end is a chimera that cannot be reached, then it must always facilitate and invite further exploration, if the Dream is not to die. Along the sides of this everyday, pragmatic stretch of road are the Dream's painted promises, of glamour, beauty and excitement, somewhere outside in America. F. Scott Fitzgerald saw this allure in travel. The love of the doomed Gatsby's life, along with her husband, travels with no apparent purpose in pursuit of an ever-receding dream:

> They had spent a year in France for no particular reason, and then drifted here and there unrestfully wherever people played polo and were rich together. I felt Tom would drift on forever seeking, a little wistfully, for the dramatic turbulence of some irrecoverable football game. (Fitzgerald 1994: 12)

Along with Fitzgerald, Evans looks askance at the American Dream and, for a moment, beneath its glittering mantle, glimpses a cloven hoof. Evans' comfortable, unremarkable houses, with their presumably comfortable, unremarkable people, cannot stand in the way of the road and the Hollywood heaven it cradles. Are they a justifiable sacrifice? Evans asks at what price is the Dream pursued. Is the replacement of real lives, however humble, with the signifiers of a life that does not and cannot exist in the grey light of Atlanta acceptable? He asks whether America has counted the cost.[1]

European travellers had mostly marvelled at the American highway, however. Some saw the road as the defining aspect of American culture. Only a year after Evans' *American Photographs* was published, the Russians Ilf and Petrov wrote:

> America is located on a large Automobile Highway. When we shut our eyes and try to resurrect in memory the country, we see before us not Washington, not New York, not San Francisco, not hills, not factories, not canyons but the crossing of two roads and a gasoline station against the background of telegraph wires and advertising billboards. Roads are one of the most remarkable phenomena in American life. (Ilf and Petrov 1937: 76–89)

Wolfgang Koeppen, in his *American Journey*, so closely resembles Frank's account of the car that his work could serve as a summary of its role in *The Americans*:

> This garden wrested from the wilderness seemed to be inhabited less by humans than by automobiles. Motor vehicles dominated the landscape, stood in flocks before each house, camped in forest clearings, promenaded along the rivers, had their own drive in restaurants and theatre in the open field, their own hotels and huge immensely melancholy cemeteries. It was the automobiles that seemed to be lords of this continent. (Koeppen 1959: 45–46)

While the road may serve as a signifier of journey, associated with concepts of time, space and longing, Frank is intent on interrogating Koeppen's 'lords of the continent'. He examines the Americans' automobile existence and watches their rites of passage, with the car as conduit. Fifties Europe was, by comparison, relatively car free. A Swiss could not help but wonder at the easy colonization of so much of life by such alien technology.

The car supplies *The Americans* with one of its most powerful narrative devices. Frank's automobile photographs echo something of the approach of Edward Steichen's *The Family of Man* exhibition, mounted in New York in 1955, in which Frank was featured. This display of 503 photographs by 257 photographers from 68 countries was the apogee of 'humanistic photography', and followed the chronology of a life (Johnson 1989: 37). After courtship comes birth, childhood and family. These are followed by mature years of working, eating, making music, dancing and studying. Courtship comes again for the progeny of the previously depicted coupling. Old age and death follow. Frank's images mirror this existence and 'feed back' on Steichen's conventional view.

In *Public park, Ann Arbor, Michigan* semi-naked couples lie entwined between the vehicles that brought them to this place. The car at centre shot, with its door wide open, is at most a yard from its mating occupants. Parked on grass, the cars reflect the brilliance of the light between and behind the trees that surround them. The couples prefer the proximity of their vehicles to the brilliant clearing behind. What once was a wander in the forest, falling into grass in summer's blissful heat and silence, as in Bill Brandt's *Forgetting it All* (B. Brandt, estate of B. Brandt) from *A Camera in London*, published in 1948, is now its simulacrum, a dash to a forest carpark and a fumble between the cars before dashing back to the pressing needs of the day. This irresistible pressure of time, facilitated by the automobile, is echoed by Kerouac in *On the Road*: 'Boys and girls in America have such a sad time together; sophistication demands that they submit to sex immediately without proper preliminary talk' (Kerouac 1972: 57). The cars stand unregarded by their otherwise occupied owners, appearing at first glance to be the guardians of this vulnerable and intimate moment. Frank has foreshortened his composition, creating a confusion of naked bodies and car parts. This lends the cars a looming, possessive quality. The classic '50s 'face' designs for the car fronts suggest a threatening, alien presence. The front bumper of the central car carries two vertical bosses, which look like tusks or fangs. Without question the youth of America include their vehicles in the rituals of courtship. This product of mass production silently watches the process of human production. This technological creation is included in the ceremony of procreation. The car is there at the moment of conception.

The Family of Man allowed nothing as unseemly as an automobile to compromise the intimacy of the private space of lovers. In its photographs couples kiss and cuddle in streets and parks. If technology is present, it is never more than an abandoned bicycle, as in Gotthard Schuh's picture (Museum of Modern Art, New York), or the blurred image of a background train (E. Haas, collection of the Magnum agency). The focus is in the mystery, the wonder and joy of this intimacy. The photographs echo the pounding of blood in the ears of their subjects. Frank instead examines the context. His image is compromised, anti-ideal. Its black, mass-produced automobiles embody too much reality. Whether or not this image is palatable, whether it represents 'good taste' and the niceties of the public who viewed *The Family of Man* in droves, is not the issue for Frank. It is reality.

Frank continues his life story with *Motorama – Los Angeles.* Three children sit inside a car. One is behind the wheel while two others occupy the rear seat. Like their older siblings in the park, there is no sense of question in these children's faces. They accept entirely the place of this lump of technology in their childhood world. Their interior is brightly lit, surrounded by a world in darkness. There is the suggestion of protection. Steve Fitch in *Diesels and Dinosaurs* remembers this sense:

> Certain objects would acquire a symbolic—even ritualistic—stature in my still unfashioned psyche. The Buick itself became an icon of sorts: to me it was a landed fish, a large benevolent animal. Sitting in it was like riding in the belly of a whale. The world outside the car was dangerous and obscure. Everything was bent and mysterious. I felt akin to an explorer on another planet. (Fitch 1976: 42)

The concentration of light and the photograph's crisp shadows suggest the use of flash. Frank thus highlights the comfort and ease of the children in the car against the uncertain darkness outside. They, like Fitch, ride the belly of a whale. This manipulation does not amount in itself to an indication of intentionality on Frank's part. His later selection of this image with its dramatic tonal contrasts does.

Later in *The Americans*, Frank revisits this theme. *Butte, Montana* pictures a portly, older woman filling the front seat of a car, with several children crammed in the back. Neither the car nor their clothing is down-at-heel, yet there is a homely workaday feel about them, which contrasts with the earlier photograph. Frank is revealing different American children from very different places, stuck in the back of cars. Their cars, like their clothes and their towns, signal their wealth and their perception of social status. Cars are included in the signals of social stratification.

The automobile was present at the moment of creation, during childhood and during the intoxicating summer of youthful love. The car is, for Frank's Americans, an unquestioned adjunct to existence, accepted at its core, as necessary as air.

Frank continues his investigation with an observation of the exuberance of young people in *Belle Isle – Detroit.* Black youths look with curiosity out of a big black cabriolet as it rushes past, the background blurred by the necessary movement of his camera. *Belle Isle* visually echoes an untitled Ralph Crane photograph from *The Family of Man* (collection of Black Star). In Crane's image, a group of well-dressed young whites careens down a road. Frank records the black equivalents of Crane's adolescents, a colour rarely seen enjoying leisure in Steichen's exhibition. *Belle Isle* is immediately followed by *Detroit,* a photograph of a nervous, white-haired Caucasian couple sitting in a stationary car, staring at something out of frame. Their white sedan is roofed over, a protection from the exterior that, judging by their expressions, they welcome. Frank juxtaposes a black cabriolet with a white sedan, a black family with a plenitude of children and an old white couple with none, and contrasts movement with stasis. Open-topped youthful exuberance precedes the roofed-over defensiveness of age.

Cabriolets and sedans feature further in *Drive in Movie – Detroit.* Frank shot this photograph at dusk, stooping to the eye level of the cars' occupants. He preserves a sense of space by firing down an empty alley between cars. The outdoor cine-screen appears small, occupying approximately a sixth of the space filled by the evening sky. The position of Frank's camera and the focal length of its lens render the plaid-shirted actors little larger than their audience. The array of cars locked on to this little screen is contrasted with the expanse of sky. America curves huge and featureless behind the movie. Do they see this? Perhaps it would be too disturbing. Staying in their cars and focusing on themselves and their culture, reflected on the screen, is the best way to ignore this immensity. Frank's technical fastidiousness is exampled by this image. The name of the drive-in cinema is backwards, suggesting he has reversed the image. Although it is possible that the name is designed to be read from the rear of the screen, this would be unusual.[2]

As a contrast to these occupied youths, making out and watching movies, *U.S. 91, leaving Blackfoot, Idaho* pictures two intent young men, perhaps a little older, yet still wide-eyed and fresh-faced. They stare through the car's windshield and out of frame at the road ahead. Their expressions suggest intensity of purpose, a full engagement with the issues and concerns of their lives. They are racing to meet their tomorrow in some small town, some diner, or at some crossroads. The exterior world is burned out, brilliant white against the shady intimacy of the interior. This again describes the vehicle as a version of home, an extension of the dark warmth of womb or bed, the red comfort of the inside of our eyes. Unusually for *The Americans*, we know the story of this image. Kerouac, in his introduction, wrote:

> Robert picks up two hitch hikers and lets them drive the car, at night, and people look at their two faces looking grimly onward into the night ('Visionary Indian angels who were visionary Indian angels' says Allen Ginsberg) and people say 'Ooo how mean they look' but all they want to do is arrow on down that road and get back to the sack—Robert here tells us so… (Kerouac, in Frank 1959: 6)

The image is obviously not at night, but the intent hitchhikers are familiar. This mode of travelling was popular with Beat generation artists, and has remained controversial, retaining an image of recklessness and danger. Kerouac, in one of many descriptions of hitchhiking, writes: 'Here the big trucks roared, wham, and inside two minutes one of them cranked to a stop for me. I ran for it with my soul whoopeeing' (Kerouac 1972: 16). These intent young Americans appear to silently 'whoopee' as they gun Frank's car into the night, drawing always nearer to the promise of comfort, warmth, food. This idea of the road-as-intoxication was also a theme for Kerouac:

> How that truck disposed of the Nebraska nub—the nub that sticks out over Colorado! And soon I realized I was actually at last over Colorado. I yelled for joy. We passed the bottle. The great blazing stars came out, the far receding sand hills got dim. I felt like an arrow that could shoot out all the way. (Kerouac 1972: 27)

Frank is considering the energy of young men, their drive, ambition and focus. They are at the wheel in a world dominated by the car, passionately hurtling toward the destiny of themselves and of their world, minds and bodies engaged in their activity. There is a slight undertone of apprehension in their faces, a barely visible uncertainty. This shadow is entirely appropriate to Frank's purpose. His purposeful, physical-prime driver follows his chosen path with vigour, yet is hounded by the spectre of self-doubt, haunted by the knowledge that his course may be ill-advised and may result, ultimately, in irremediable failure.

Frank fills the following page with *St. Petersburg, Florida.* Withered old people sit back to back on benches. This is Main Street, Small Town, USA. Above their wizened faces and array of crisp but dubiously tasteful outfits, a long finned duotone sedan cruises by, blurred by its speed. Is this the vehicle of the intent young men? These ancient Americans lack any of the conviction or urgency of their juniors; their lives have been pretty much lived and their actions have led to this appearance of peaceful passivity. They do not sit in cars, their desire for speed, perhaps, a thing of the past. They are oblivious to the passage of the young men, at such a different place in their lives. Kerouac was again inspired to comment in his introduction:

> St. Petersburg Florida the retired old codgers on a bench in the busy mainstreet … As American a picture—the faces don't editorialize or criticize or say anything but "This is the way we are in real life and if you don't like it I don't know anything about it 'cause I'm living my own life my way and may God bless us all, mebbe" … "if we deserve it"(Kerouac, in Frank 1959: 6)

Backyard – Venice West, California takes the point further. An ancient old man sits beneath a cobbled-together striped canopy, resembling the American flag. Surrounded by huge vegetables and scrub trees, this garden wrested from the wilderness sits behind a single-storey, white-painted board house. Between bungalow and old man is a derelict car. Its paint is peeling, boxes sit on its roof and a garden hoe leans against it. The 'steed' of this retired knight errant is likewise retired. The conduit of his great and glorious deeds, whatever they may have been, is incorporated into his retirement garden with him. As he hangs up his spurs, so his car, the essential partner to his exploits, is decommissioned. Frank's composition captures the brilliant Californian light leaping from every surface in this image. It describes the vitality of the world. The old man hides from it under his canopy and the corrupted paintwork of the fading car refuses to shine. They are passing beyond this light to another place.

The rites of passage are again remembered in *Funeral – St. Helena, South Carolina.* This photograph figures suited and hatted mourners, standing in a circle amongst their cars, watching the proceedings. Two of the men, intent perhaps on the address, lean on a black car, their faces mournful. There is no perception of incongruity. The car is there at conception; it is there at commitment to the ground. There is nothing of the serenity of *The Family of Man's* idealized descriptions of the rites of death. None of that exhibition's photographs of ceremonies from around the world include anything so prosaic or coldly functional as a sedan. None of the mourners wears such a resigned and ambivalent expression.

Frank has measured out a life in Cadillacs and Chevrolets, but does not end his analysis there. As well as conduit, the car is also an icon, as important in America's new materialist religion as the flag, the jukebox or the gas station. Frank also examines those occasions when the car transcends the material and approaches the divine.

Chicago is a photograph of the rear of a polished black automobile. The car reflects a distorted image of high city blocks straddled by a filigree of girders. Behind all this, taking up perhaps a fifth of the composition, is the reflected sky, so often wide and empty but here restrained and distant between the masonry and observed only in the distorting mirror of an automobile's rear end. The number plate tells us where and when: 'Land of Lincoln, 19 Illinois 56'. This photograph provides a concise, idiosyncratic portrait of a city. It doesn't stop there, however. The rear window carries a plaque, stuck up with tape, that tells us, 'Christ died for our sins'. Another, fastened to the number plate, reads 'Christ came to save sinners'. The car is a pulpit, considered an appropriate vessel to carry the sacred messages of humanity, incorporated entirely into spiritual life. Henri Cartier-Bresson's 1947 photograph *Tennessee* (estate of H. Cartier-Bresson) is a superb prefigured variation of Frank's theme. Bresson examines, with typically wry humour, the bizarre visual relationship between religion and the automobile, as Frank would do nine years later. Bresson pictures a white cross, carved with the words 'Jesus is coming soon', standing in front of a house in a valley, surrounded by trees. Its importance is heightened by its position at the intersection of both vertical and horizontal golden section lines. Behind the cross, in this palpably peaceful place, lies a rusting collection of wrecked cars. The cemetery 'feel' is heightened by a wreath-like plant, growing amidst the grave-like mounds in the foreground. Is this really a Christian burial ground for cars?

St. Francis, gas station and City Hall – Los Angeles depicts the saint holding aloft a cross in the dusky light of early morning or late evening (this is not St Francis, in fact, as we will discuss in the third section of this book. Frank chose this appellation, whether erroneously or by design is open to question). In his other hand is a small church, not as many viewers and writers believe a bible. He preaches directly across a deserted highway, into the sun. Behind the gas station opposite, advertising 'Atlas tires' and 'Lubrication' is a huge lot filled with what appears to be hundreds of parked cars. St Francis is famous for his sermon to the birds. In his *Canticle of the Sun*, he called the moon 'sister' and the sun 'brother'. Here he preaches to an audience of automobiles. The statue stands in oppressively undifferentiated shadow, *contre jour*.

St. Francis follows *Mississippi River, Baton Rouge, Louisiana*. Here a black priest, in brilliant white ecclesiastical robe and hat, kneels before the river. He also holds a book and a high white cross but has, additionally, a tambourine. His posture echoes that of 'Francis', save that he is kneeling. His locale could not be more different. Surrounded by grass, he rests on cardboard. Nearby, some kind of fabric is held down by stones, exciting curiosity as to what it might cover. Shadows on his robes indicate an early or late hour. The overwhelming impression is of sunset. His supplication is across the huge river facing into the sun. What mystery is he enacting, what soul poetry does he read to the evening, unheard, unregarded? While 'Francis', frozen in stone, expostulates silently to the myriad cars and to Sunset Boulevard, here at the heart of America, oblivious to the regard of others, be they individual or corporate, a priest from an unknown order reads his quiet liturgy to the wide land and inevitable sunset. The power of this image inspired Kerouac to include it in the first paragraph of his introduction:

> …mysteries like the Negro priest squatting underneath the bright liquid belly mer of the Mississippi at Baton Rouge for some reason at dusk or early dawn with a white snowy cross and secret incantations never known outside the bayou … (Kerouac, in Frank 1959: 5)

This comparison is entirely unflattering for car-ridden Los Angeles. The serene, car-free clarity of *Baton Rouge* stands sharply against the grey, smog-bound city morning. Modern white America is Frank's victim and the car its symptom.[3]

Crosses on scene of highway accident – U.S. 91, Idaho and *Assembly line – Detroit* consider heaven and hell. Frank's refusal in them to entirely abhor or entirely embrace the highway and its life is important. It is rarely possible to be prescriptive or certain, especially with these 'holy mysteries'. Frank often sought nothing so resolutely as to image and imply the transcendent and indescribable. *Crosses on scene of highway accident* is a beautiful example of this. Frank photographed a road flanked by three simple white crosses, an image that reads as a memorial to three road accident victims. It is followed by *Assembly line – Detroit*, a car factory staffed by oily, busy line workers, an image of the inception of that which caused the victims' destruction. Men create cars to facilitate life, which then, on occasions, destroy it. Life and death exist within this complex relationship.

Streaming from the top of *Crosses on scene of highway accident* is a flare of light. It recalls an austere, ascetic rendering of a renaissance heaven and earth, the host of heaven above the material plane. The shaft of white light above the markers contrasts sharply with the dirty grays of the factory that follows, this latter having an infernal suggestion. Frank conjures heaven and hell in the almost invisible space between his pictures. He discusses the possibility of release from earthly drudgery—signified by the factory—that death brings, a return to the divine.

Covered car – Long Beach, California is the apogee of Frank's consideration of the car as a holy object. At the same time, it examines the importance of the automobile for the mature American. A car stands in front of an unimpressive house. It is single-storey, blank concrete with tiny windows and a couple of ventilators in the wall. It could easily be a factory or garage, if not for the number '20' fixed to the door and, further to the right, fastened on to the fence. A small lantern above the number also suggests that this is a habitation. In front of the house, two thick palm trees stand, like the columns of a Greek temple. Their leaves meet overhead against the sky, suggesting a portico. Between these trees is a parked car covered with a shining white cloth, either silk or a modern synthetic. The shape of headlights, aerial, roof and tail fins are just discernible beneath the cloth. The car is altar like, waiting for prayer or sacrifice. It is cosseted in a way that the house, certainly, is not. If the owner of the car is the owner of the house, as is assumed, then it is obvious which of these objects is their passion. The road and its potentialities represent more than the sedentary, humble house and deserve, therefore, more care, more reverence. This image is the apotheosis of Evans' *Frame Houses, Atlanta*, discussed earlier. Evans' warning about the mesmerising fallacy of the dream of the road has here flowered into full-blown adulation of the road and car, perhaps the American Dream's most convincing materialization.

Frank soberly acknowledges the sacrifices demanded by this automobile altar in his next image, *Car accident – U.S. 66, between Winslow and Flagstaff, Arizona.* Four people stand in rain or snow cautiously staring at a cloth, covering what may be assumed to be corpses. The composition unmistakably echoes the preceding image, the palm trees replaced by onlookers, the silk-covered car by tarpaulin-covered bodies. A couple of humble buildings stand in the middle distance, behind them the expanse of America cut only by telegraph posts and cables. The whole image is of the most melancholy, monotonous grey. Only some of the clothing and the inside of two buildings feature any darker tone. This is in stark contrast to *Covered car – Long Beach, California,* photographed in bright sunlight with crisp shadows and saturated tones, sooty blacks and brilliant whites. The certainty of those lives, the order and satisfaction of everything in its place, everything protected, contrasts with these random deaths, on a gray day, on an unremarkable stretch of highway, in nowhere in particular. American adults both cherish their cars and are killed by them: as is so often suggested in the art and literature of the American Dream, they are the victims of that which they love. Frank uses again the style of his pictures to reinforce their theme. Without these defining gestures his intent would be clouded.

What, then, is Frank's conclusion? Many of his images are obviously critical. Hatred and criticism of the car were common amongst contemporary commentators. Charles Merz, writing before Frank set out, described the pointlessness of recreational driving:

> Impressions? Yes. Impressions of a never-ending road … Thrills? Yes. Thrills of scenery that would be worth stopping for if only there were time … Trophies? Yes. Trophies to bring back memories of this day of travel: postcards, toy balloons and paper bathing girls … Yet surely these are poor rewards for so much travel. Surely it is worth no man's while to drive three hundred miles from break of dawn on Sunday just to add another pennant to his string, or to hurry half the day for the apparent purpose of arriving at a point far enough away to make it necessary to turn at once and hurry home again. (Merz 1928: 19–20)

Frank is far more ambivalent than this. The car is protection in a Motorama as much as a killer in Flagstaff, liberation for the young men leaving Blackfoot as much as a fetish in *Covered Car*.

Frank sees what Merz figured without. Travel is a metaphor for change. It is the signifier of progress, of movement, the constant incremental approach towards the gates of paradise. Frank clearly echoed this in *U.S. 285 – New Mexico*. For people tied to endless repetitive work and a daily struggle for survival, like the women in *Parade – Hoboken, New Jersey*, travel, even for one day a week, could represent an escape from the dreariness of everyday life. It is not a real escape, merely a symbol, a representation. It is no less significant for this. Many Americans in the '50s spent their lives working in coal pit or steel-mill, shipyard, shop or automobile plant. They sacrificed their youth and strength for poor wages and the slow growth of the US economy, finally to retire briefly and die. For them, this simulacrum was as essential as food or warmth. They needed this dream. The pennants at which Merz jeers contain, in their tawdry kitsch, the hopes of another, better, life. The memory of those few free-feeling Sunday hours sustained days of drudgery. We still, of course, live with this reality.

Frank sees that for Americans the car and highway represent even more than this. In their living memory, theirs was the land of frontiers and pioneers, exploring an unknown world, with always the possibility of striking gold or claiming acres of fertile virgin land, bereft by the bullet of their First Nation stewards. By the middle years of the twentieth century, the country was consolidating its expansion. Journeys that had involved danger, adventure and promise had become safe, sanitized and, by comparison, fruitless. The everyday life of the Americans no longer necessitated travel. For a nation so peopled by refugees, prospectors, runaways and dreamers, both religious and philosophical, this change could only be deeply traumatic. The Pacific was reached, the interior surveyed, the Indians 'pacified', or, more accurately, annihilated. There was nowhere new to explore or to escape to. The loss of real adventure had to be replaced with an aesthetic simulacrum. It became symbolized in the thrill of a journey to some theme park or 'discovery cave', as the former were known in embryo. The pursuit of the Dream could no longer be invested in the mythical frontier, lived vicariously through pulp fiction, the newspapers or travelling Wild West shows. The Frontier no longer existed. The echoes of the constitutional right of every American to engage in the pursuit of life, love and liberty, to bear arms and to be 'free' became, in the light of factory work, the imperative of poverty and the control of an ever more regimented society, a constant searching. They yearned for the time and place, on a Sunday afternoon, of course, and within easy reach of home, when truth and beauty would finally integrate in the harmonious music of the spheres, played as accompaniment to the ultimate orgasmic sensory overload. They searched for something that would change their lives forever, the echo of what Frank describes as 'where God is' (Frank 1991: after plate 63) or Kerouac saw as the moment when 'the pearl would be handed to me' (Kerouac 1972: 11).

Frank counted the cost of the highway and the car while celebrating their metaphors. He travelled these prescribed asphalt paths in pursuit of their promise, aware that it may be spurious. He pressed these simulacrums into service as signifiers of the journey within, sharing the hope of so many whose writing was never read, whose photographs were never seen. Many of these anonymous Americans pursuing their Sunday afternoon Dream were also aware of its chimerical nature, appearing to form for a moment from the heat haze or distant fog into the gates of paradise, only to dissolve again into nothing. One moment saw a flare of light over three crosses speaking of heaven, the next only a deserted desert road, fading sticks of wood stuck in the dirt.

The book's final image, *U.S. 90, en route to Del Rio, Texas*, shows a woman and child asleep in the passenger seat of a car. The black automobile is pulled up at the side of the road, its nearside headlight lit. The peaceful sleeping faces are almost a Madonna and child. The nearness of the car to the viewer and the eye-level angle suggest intimacy. The subjects' occupation of the passenger seat leaves no doubt that this is Frank's family. A sidelong view of the same car, taken in 1956 but not included in *The Americans*, confirms this. It is titled *Andrea, Pablo, Mary, Texas, 1956*. The passengers are identifiably the same as those in *U.S. 90, en route to Del Rio, Texas*. In this portrait of his family, Frank identified himself with car culture. He equated his own experience with that of all those others he had depicted. He embraced that upon which he had sophisticatedly commented, accepting it as part of his life also. The car and the pantheon of American signs are part of the experience contained in these photographs, the conduit of his journey and the views from its window. This is his confessional, finally turning the camera upon himself and showing us his reality: another driver on another road driving around wild America looking for the 'pearl', for 'where God is'.

Notes

1. This is the contrast between *Frame Houses* and *U.S. 285*. Frank fills his image with tarmac, a road with almost no evidence of humanity, leading to an unknown but luminous destination. Evans considers the effect of the highway on the country it divides, giving it only a fifth of his composition. Frank looks along the empty miles of highway, while Evans looks across the road at the houses it isolates.

   It is crucial to see these pictures in the context of their time. Evans' work was twenty years before Frank's, a time in which the growth of the highway and its culture was a new thing. Evans is powerfully questioning this new phenomenon. Frank stepped out into a country in the full flush of highway culture, a nation no longer asking the questions to which Evans gave visual form. Frank's response cannot but be different to that of Evans. The nation had made its choice and married its own glittering, insubstantial self. Frank travels a road already laden with symbolism, its reality accepted and beyond question, its meaning and true function his subjects. The significant and overwhelming similarity in these photographs is their social function. Both photographers are attempting to figure a truth and present it to their viewers.

   The foundational importance of Walker Evans and his book *American Photographs* has been noted. Tod Papageorge explores this further in his *Walker Evans and Robert Frank: An Essay on Influence* (1981).

2. J.R. Ellerman's, *Californian Drive-In Movie* (1958, collection of *Life*) provides an interesting parallel. The composition is stunningly similar, having an eye-line running between a cabriolet and a sedan which closely resemble those in Frank's image. The eye-line is higher, but it observes a screen and sky in a similar relationship to Frank's. Ellerman's photograph appeared in *Life* in 1958, the year after Frank published pictures in *Camera* and *Pageant* magazines, and the year in which Robert Delpire published *Les Americaines* in France. The date of this photograph and Ellerman's relationship to Frank, if any, have yet to be determined. The screen in his picture shows a scene from Cecil B. de Mille's Paramount epic *The Ten Commandments* (1956), in which Moses, played by Charlton Heston, divides the Red Sea. This welding of The Bible, Hollywood heroism and Technicolor is entirely consistent with the relationship in *The Americans* between *Drive in Movie – Detroit* and the image that precedes it. This relationship is explored further in Part Three.

3. The slanted cross and the loneliness of Baton Rouge echo the skewed cross of Cartier-Bresson's *Mexico*. The grave marker, all that remains in the physical world of this extinguished life, is neglected and slowly but certainly falling to the earth,

an analogue of the return to the ground and oblivion which is everyone's destiny. The dolorous feel of Cartier-Bresson's image is aided by the wide desert land, empty of any object save the grave. This is unlike that of Frank's Negro priest. It relates much more closely to *Crosses on scene of highway accident – U.S. 91, Idaho*. Frank's work, with its implication of a shining otherworld, is, even here, more positive than Cartier-Bresson's.

8

Losing My Religion: New Icons For a New Civilization

'Icons' is a term originally applied to devotional images created and used by the Byzantine, Greek and Russian Orthodox Churches. Paintings of Christ, Mary, the Saints and other religious subjects were seen as objects of devotion and inspirations in worship. Icons were, above all else, religious works. Frank saw a religious aspect in many of the objects he photographed. He recorded jukeboxes, gas stations and a silk-covered car at the exact moment in which their function as religious objects was apparent. Frank observed that this containment and representation of the divine within the material interestingly approximates the role traditionally fulfilled by the images of religion. This is not surprising. Karl Marx wrote that

> Religion is, indeed, the self-consciousness and self-esteem of man who has either not yet won through to himself, or has already lost himself again…
>
> It is the fantastic realization of the human essence since the human essence has not acquired any true reality…
>
> Religion is the sigh of the oppressed creature, the heart of a heartless world, and the soul of soulless conditions. (Marx 1977: 127)

His argument is that religion is necessary and functional in any society or human condition that is uncertain, threatened or oppressed. America, for most of its inhabitants, was all of these things. For so many of the reasons explored already, the 50s in America was a time of deep and profound change. If Marx's necessary conditions for religion still prevailed, while the nature and conditions of civilization were changing, it follows that the emerging society needed new symbols. Frank said that he was looking for things 'in the United States that signifies the kind of civilization born here and spreading elsewhere' (Frank 1954, in Greenough 2009: 362).

A secular materialistic society needs secular material signs for the world beyond the visible, as the old signs will slowly be defiled and disfigured. Frank found this new faith in unlikely objects and places, as he identified the *credo* of the America he experienced.

Frank was also interested in recording the passing of the old. His images of older symbols of faith are sometimes ambivalent, often eviscerating and rarely entirely positive. Perhaps only the other-worldly, inscrutable black priest who Frank photographed beside the Mississippi River near Baton Rouge is imaged as worthy of his snow-white vestments and the cross he carries. *St. Francis* (who isn't really St. Francis, as we will see later) on the following page preaches to an LA highway and parking lot, appearing as an anachronism, a cry from the past, remonstrating with an oblivious America. *Chicago* sees the cross and the Saviour reduced to the subject of bumper stickers.[1] No mystery, no wild impassioned life-giving talk of eternity. Just pieces of tin, stuck on to an automobile.

Frank's imaging of the old sigils of belief is most often ironic, or critical. *Department store – Lincoln, Nebraska* pictures rows of small white crosses for sale on a store table. The sale sign reads 'Hested's. Remember your loved ones. 69 c'. At such a bargain price, these must surely be plastic. Frank reveals the value this American store, and by extension Americans, place on the cross as a memorial for loved ones: 69 cents. The jumble of boxes beneath the table promises an unlimited supply of identical tributes. The individuality of the dead will be ignored. Grief, mourning and memory are mass-facilitated. Frank's implication as per the Cross is clear. Any society that can unquestioningly reduce its hitherto most sacred symbol to this level cannot truly reverence it.

Another subtle and powerful comment on the decline of America's traditional faith is *Restaurant – U.S. 1 leaving Columbia, South Carolina*. On the most immediate level, this image is one among several pictures examining the nature and character of the American diner. This interpretation is valid: Frank chose to exclude any information as to the identity of the man on the TV in his caption. It is difficult on visual evidence alone to attribute anything to him. He is serious, perhaps even sour-faced or aggressive. Contemporary Americans may have recognized him, but the Europeans who saw *Les Americaines* probably would not have. This photograph is one of those chosen by Frank for his retrospective book *The Lines of My Hand* (Frank 1989). Here the picture carries the caption 'South Carolina, Oral Roberts on TV'. The identity of the broadcaster is significant. Roberts is one of America's most famous television evangelists, notable also as the cousin, and denouncer, of rock and roll singer and pianist Jerry Lee Lewis. Despite being well known for his Christian faith, Lewis stormed out of his cousin's church after being continually harangued for performing the 'devil's music' (McBride 1989).

Roberts is almost certainly preaching from the television in this restaurant. His face has an expression of dour sincerity, symptomatic of media evangelism. Roberts, however, preaches to no one. The diner is empty. Next to his screen daylight pours through the window, redolent of joy and excitement, burning out the photograph. Over the page, in the direction Roberts is looking, a couple sit in a convertible, in the midst of many other

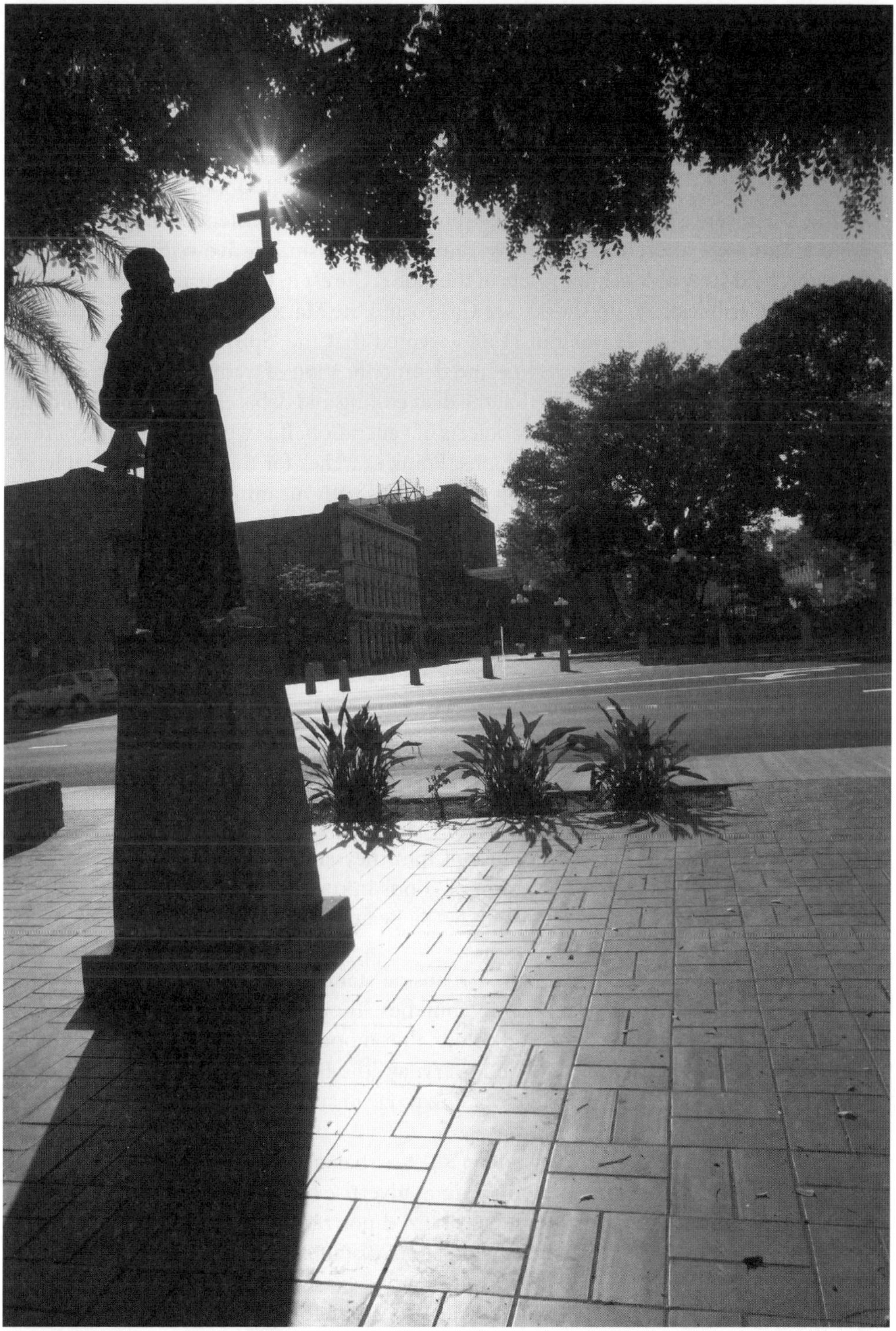

The statue which Frank included in *St Francis, gas station and City Hall – LosAngeles* is actually of St. Junipero Serra. It has been relocated and no longer looks out over Sunset Boulevard. (Photo by Jonathan Day/copyright control)

cars watching a drive-in movie. Is Frank suggesting that Roberts' potential viewers have run away to the movies? Instead of an emotional biblical exposition, even if it is delivered by new technology, the people of Frank's America prefer Hollywood.

The 1950s were a difficult time for the spirit and its world. Existentialism and scientific materialism were the creeds of many thinkers. Marxism, an avowedly anti-religious doctrine, held sway across huge tracts of the globe. Unrest in Central and South America and in the Caribbean would shortly see Castro and the Marxists in power in Cuba, right on America's doorstep. It was not at all accepted that the 'Spirit' even existed. Frank, however, having described the decline and desanctification of traditional icons, does not deny the spiritual. Instead, he sees that the discrediting and debasement of the traditional icons necessitate the creation of new objects of veneration. It is within the nature of man. In many of these *Americans* photographs, Frank searches for these new material icons. He observes the Americans investing new objects with meaning. Not everyone would see this. Again, Frank fulfils the role of artist-as-identifier.[2] He makes it his business to reveal the signs.

The new icons will not necessarily echo the old, or be located in similar places. Frank comments on this idea in *Detroit*, taken during the Fellowship but left out of *The Americans.* A place as unexpected as the roadside and an object as prosaic as a Wrigley's gum advertisement provide an insight into the needs and character of this New World and its idiosyncratic symbolic requirements. Simone de Beauvoir, writing in 1953 in *America Day by Day*, significantly another Grove Press publication, noticed:

> The average American devotes a large part of his leisure to driving along the highways; the filling stations, the roads, the hotels, the lonely inns exist only for the tourist and because of him they are profoundly American things. The shameless profusion of goods in roadside stands is a poetry as fantastic as in a Baroque church. (de Beauvoir 1953: 161)

She suggests that, for the American, a roadside stand embodies exactly that 'poetry' which in the Baroque was celebrated in churches. They fulfil the same needs in human beings, a wild celebration of form and colour, the embodiment of the glories of existence, all that is not tawdry, earth-bound and everyday. The Baroque church was the ultimate multi-sensory, multimedia experience of its day. De Beauvoir equates this with American roadside stands.

Frank photographed a set of wooden shelves, balanced on boxes, which carried a range of fresh fruit. Large hand-painted signs advertise the price of the items to passing motorists. Behind the display is a huge, stylized portrait of a smiling woman. Frank's composition creates the illusion that this large, distant face is smaller and is peering over the fruit stall with a leering, almost lecherous expression. Frank's manipulation of depth of field achieves this; both the stall and the distant billboard are in clear focus. The picture is lit by sunlight from the left front, leaving enough shadow to define the fruit shelves, while using the flatness of the light to defeat the viewer's sense of perspective. The advertisement carries the text 'Wrigley's Juicy Fruit. Delicious.' Frank depicts simultaneously the reality and its simulacrum, real fruit and a chemically manufactured, gummy symbol. One of these is advertised by homemade signs, the other by a huge, expensively printed display. It is significant which of these is on the billboard. The artificial product is attempting to subsume the identity of the real. The simulacrum, the representative symbol, the replacement, is the choice of corporate America.

The intention of this photograph, held within its clear, early light, doesn't appear to be wholly critical. It feels ironic. Somewhere between the poetry of the fruit stall and the huge Juicy Fruit advertisement is the nature of America. In its traditional cultural role, fruit represents more than mere apples and pears. It embodies all that is fresh, dew covered, juicy, wholesome, ripe. It is coloured in shades both pastel and lurid. It holds a corner of the hearts of men. The real thing, amalgamations of skin, pith and flesh, is no longer big enough, in 1950's America, to celebrate this beautiful vision. Wrigley can do it better, on billboards the size of orchards. This new technological world is bigger, thanks to hormones; brighter, thanks to beta-carotene; and better tasting, thanks to monosodium glutamate.

Frank was not the first commentator to explore the significance of these huge American paint and paper faces. In *The Great Gatsby*, F. Scott Fitzgerald describes one such billboard:

> ...above the grey land and the spasms of bleak dust which drift endlessly over it, you perceive, after a moment, the eyes of Doctor T.J. Eckleburg. The eyes are blue and gigantic, their retinas are one yard high. They look out of no face, but, instead, from a pair of enormous yellow spectacles. His eyes dimmed a little by many paintless days, brood on over the solemn dumping ground. (Fitzgerald 1994: 29)

Fitzgerald's vision has none of the ironic ambivalence of Frank's *Detroit*. The eyes become a looming representative of a dark, arcane presence. They are America as a semiotic sign, the American dream personified. The advertisement that once was a dream of wealth and prosperity, brightly painted, is now peeling above the remaining refuse: 'Over the ash heaps the giant eyes of Doctor T.J. Eckleburg kept their vigil' (Fitzgerald 1994: 29). The common criticism of Frank as 'anti-American' is clearly denied here. Fitzgerald is far more critical of his own country. Frank reveals strangeness, irony and comedy in his image of the roadside.

If Simone de Beauvoir saw something nearly divine, churchlike, iconic in the 'fantastic poetry' observed beside the American highway, writer James Agee saw something similar in the vernacular houses and furnishings of poor Southern share-croppers. In 1936 he collaborated with Walker Evans, producing their book *Let Us Now Praise Famous Men* at the commission of *Fortune* magazine (published 1941). One of the photographs in this work is *Church Organ and Pews*. As has been noted, images of traditional faith held little attraction for Frank, except in exposés of their compromise. There is a mystical quality in Evans' photograph though, which is taken up by Frank in his imaging of jukeboxes. Agee attempts to describe this quality:

> There can be more beauty and more deep wonder in the standings and spacings of mute furnishings on a bare floor between the squaring bourns of walls than in any music ever made: that this square home as it stands in unshadowed earth between the winding years of heaven, is, not to me but of itself, one among the serene and final uncapturable beauties of existence. (Agee and Evans 1941: 24)

The richly carved harmonium in Evans' picture evidences this. It stands in a space at the front of the church. Nothing impinges on it, giving it a monumental feeling. It stands alone, separated by its nature, set apart for some special purpose. It is brightly lit from a source out of shot to the left. It is radiant within the subdued light of the church. Behind the instrument is another window, its brightness almost halo like. This is a revered object in truth: Evans has composed his photograph to emphasise this.[3]

Kerouac, in his introduction to *The Americans*, sensed the importance of Frank's photographs of jukeboxes:

> After seeing these pictures you end up finally not knowing any more whether a jukebox is sadder than a coffin. That's because he's always taking pictures of jukeboxes and coffins. (Kerouac, in Frank 1959: 5)

Bar, New York City closely follows Evans' composition, although the church is replaced by the eponymous bar. The traditional meeting place for worship is replaced by a space for revelry. The room is, as in Evans' work, dimly lit, though the sense in Frank's image is nocturnal. In the centre stands a jukebox. It is not lit by daylight from a window. There is no suggestion of radiance falling on this object. It is fired from within, its own electric light far outshining anything else in the room. It glows with a white light, the traditional pictorial attribute of angels, saints and the Holy Spirit. The brilliance of the light has burned the photograph out. It spills beyond the jukebox into the surrounding air. It is uncertain whether this is due to Frank's exposure, to the printing of the image or even perhaps to the damaged lens he is thought to have chosen when he wanted flare on the film (Tucker and Brookman 1986). In any case, Frank has given the jukebox a halo.

Like the harmonium, the jukebox is imaged as a sacred object. It holds within the songs it plays the hopes and aspirations of America. In the lyrics of its contained records, as previously in the words of the sacred songs and psalms, live the dreams of the people who feed it coins. Heaven, romance, happiness and a better world are all a nickel away. It holds the new 'hymns'. The harmonium and its ancient words and tunes, in Frank's America, have had their day.

The argument for Frank's beatification of the jukebox, his proposal that its iconic status be acknowledged, is strengthened by three other examinations of this object. In *Café – Beaufort, South Carolina*, a black baby lies on a cushion close beside an ornate, black plastic and shining-metal jukebox. The box is huge in relation to the child, looming over it. Its monolithic presence is ambivalent. As with the car in *Motorama – Los Angeles*, discussed earlier, there is no certainty as to whether this technology is protective or threatening. It is unquestionably alien. The building in Frank's picture has the same homemade feel as the church in Margaret Bourke-White's *Exminster, South Carolina*. This heightens the strangeness of this high-gloss industrial object. The box is self-contained, mobile, its mechanism obscure, containing no user serviceable parts. It is from another place, another's mind, yet completely accepted. Frank's composition reveals a mother who is entirely comfortable leaving her unattended child in its care. In a corner of this low-tech, light filled room, this Rockola is so different from the bare-boards café and the flesh and blood baby as to almost require reverence. It is like the mouthpiece of a distant world, the gift of some obscure deity to the faithful. It is the high-tech inheritor of the megaphones built into the masks of Ancient Greek actors, the amplifying acoustics of a Gothic Cathedral or the shaman observed in Africa talking to the Gods through a disconnected telephone. The jukebox's songs carry the dogma of the New World, the new way. The venue is a café, not a church, a prophecy, perhaps, of the primacy-to-come of McDonald's over Methodism, the golden arches replacing the gothic arches as the people's meeting place of choice.

Bar – Las Vegas, Nevada examines another interior lit brilliantly through its windows. There is nothing here that is homemade or homespun, however. Damaged linoleum covers the large, empty floor, with only a suggestion of furniture in the shadows at extreme left breaking the desolation. Against the right-hand wall, a jukebox, looking more like a lathe than anything religious, is the object of the rapt attention of the only person in the image. He is a dark man, light reflecting off his Brylcreemed hair, his casual flowered shirt signalling his leisure. He stands in obvious communion with the box: it is his companion, his associate. If he presses a button it will provide its comforting, well-known stock answers to the questions implicit in the language of his stance.

Candy store – New York City contrasts with *Bar – Las Vegas* in that the jukebox within is surrounded by young people. A gloriously ornate example, the *Mother of Plastic*, is absorbed into the range of expressions on these adolescent faces: uncertainty, aggression, the look of hope or sadness of which Frank was so fond. Kerouac again recognized the significance of this American scene:

> I walked into the least likely place in the world, a kind of lonely plains soda fountain for the local teenage girls and boys. They were dancing a few of them, to the music of the jukebox. (Kerouac 1972: 32)

The Wurlitzer has become an adjunct to adolescence, an essential aspect of the rites of passage of the youth of 1950s America. The jukebox, however bizarre it may appear, with its shining metal and obscure swirls and fins, is not isolated but absorbed without question into the world of these teenagers. It performs for them, creating a concert, another world that they experience behind their eyes. Emphasizing this, the youth at the bottom right of *Candy store* solos on an imagined trumpet, absorbed by his inner vision. The box is a three-dimensional realization of this strange and wonderful inner America, usually only glimpsed in two-dimensional movies, or on billboards. Here it is solid and tangible, the box relished and cherished for what it embodies, more significant than the tawdry candy bar in which it sits. It is, in the imaginations of these youths, more real. Frank's photograph records the movement of an invisible power, which hangs unseen yet apparent at the centre of this picture. Ulrich Keller sees these images as depictions of poverty. He argues that:

> What makes his (Frank's) calculation of the wealth and deficit of … culture so poignant is the recognition that ultimately its material lavishness translated into human poverty, the poverty of technologically colonized minds. (Keller 1986: 23)

The question of colonization is certainly powerful in these images. Frank has chosen situations that highlight the strangeness of these machines, and their ready acceptance by humanity. Are they, though, any more strange than Catholic statues of Christ, his red Sacred Heart exposed, or Mantegna's *St. Sebastian* (1470, Louvre, Paris) stuck by arrows or Bellini's *The Ecstasy of St Theresa of Avila* (1645, Santa Maria della Vittoria, Rome)? For Frank, 'material lavishness' does not necessarily equate with poverty. In *Candy store*, the technology actualizes the dreams, this escape heightened by the ugliness of the environment, emphasized by the shining pomp in which these cogs and motors are contained. 'The sigh' as we have mentioned, 'of the oppressed creature … who has not yet won though to himself' (Marx 1977: 127).

If a Wurlitzer is a strange object with which to define a culture, then a petrol pump is surely stranger. *The Americans* responds to a sophisticated culture with sophistication. *Santa Fe, New Mexico* exists within, and responds to, a well-established genre in American photography. Many gas station pictures were taken for commercial purposes. Photographers working for Standard Oil's Picture File, which we will examine in more detail in Chapter 10, produced a plethora of such photographs. Standard Oil's images, understandably, are almost always of clean, well-maintained stations, manned by enthusiastic smiling staff. Rosskam's *Lee's Grizzly Station, Cut Bank, Montana; August 1944* (Standard Oil Archive, University of Louisville) is a small-town station in which a young woman checks a customer's tyre. Large interstate services are also featured, sitting beneath huge 'Esso' signs. Unsurprisingly, there are always cars, lights and activity. America is figured as a working nation, driving itself into the future on the power of Esso petroleum, facilitated by Esso's dedicated servants. The Russian satirists Ilf and Petrov, writing in 1937, supported this. When stopping for gas, they were impressed by the technology. They watched the pump count 'automatically the number of gallons swallowed by our automobile. With each new gallon the apparatus gave off a melodic ring.' More than this, they were enchanted by the ritual: 'Only then did the great American service begin', as the attendant moved to 'lift the hood of the machine and to test the level of the oil in the motor with a calibrated metallic ruler. If it is necessary to add oil he brings it in a handsome tin can or a tall wide necked bottle. All this is quickly done but without any fuss, and it does not cost the traveller a single cent' (Ilf and Petrov 1937: 76–89).

Frank's *Santa Fe* is as accurate as any of Standard Oil's images, yet its import is entirely other. The fuel is 'Shamrock', represented on the pumps by this Irish symbol of hope and good fortune. The huge neon sign, dwarfing every other feature of the station, reads 'Save Gas'. However 'Gas' is not illuminated and is barely visible, leaving only a giant 'Save' written across the sky. Against an empty landscape, a wide undulation with a scattering of scrub trees and a huge New Mexican sky, this pocket of civilization is literally a beacon to any petrol-hungry motorist, navigating the wastes of the semi-desert.[4] It offers salvation from a stranding in the wilderness; the station is a step in the claiming of this wild, strange land for humankind. Here, Frank has found the new frontier, no wild beasts or painted 'hostiles', as the US Army called the First Americans who didn't do as they were told, but the equally wild and savage strangeness of the desert at dusk. Mankind is now exploring an inner wilderness, a fear of loneliness, a sense of displacement.

Frank has chosen a sky illuminated from below the horizon, either at dawn or dusk. This half-light, this time of change, is redolent of an ancient human fear. The onset of darkness handicaps visual beings, who are no longer able to see an approaching enemy or predator. The emphasized horizon draws a stark line between desert and sky, a line that bisects the circular pump tops, drawing the viewer immediately to them. The pumps are slightly anthropomorphic, their illuminated discs head-like, sitting on human-sized shoulders, hoses hanging like arms. Five similar pumps stand mutely in the dirt. The station feels deserted, like something ancient, abandoned. The nearest pump is corroded at its base, marked by time. They are monolithic, immovable. They stand in an almost circle, henge-like. A Callanish or Avebury for a new culture.

In its feeling of abandonment, its lack of living humanity, this image is timeless. Vachon's photograph for Standard Oil, *Farm house and gasoline pump, Brown County, S.D.; January, 1948* (Standard Oil Archive, University of Louisville), achieves a similar, though less-focused, sensation. His petrol pump, like Frank's, stands isolated and incongruous. These photographs have become the record of the artefacts of a past civilization, as strange as Stonehenge, as mute as a sarsen. Frank is showing us the enigmatic signs which this American culture has created. They may, like the once-functional pyramids, become the way in which it is remembered. Could the obscure purpose of a stone circle or the meaning of a hieroglyph be any more extraordinary than these desert pumps, with their Shamrock signs, beneath an enormous neon 'Save'? This image speaks timelessly of the marks made by humanity on its world, the detritus of civilization. Even this vital, strange and occasionally sinister new world will also one day pass into obscurity, leaving only a random few of its symbols behind.

The notion of technology as a memorial was examined by director Fred Wilcox in MGM's *Forbidden Planet*, released in 1956 at the same time that Frank was taking these photographs. The film adapts Shakespeare's *The Tempest*, and tells of a shipwrecked scientist who discovers an ancient alien mechanism, which he reactivates. The vast machine in the film stands as a mute inscrutable monument to its creators. Significantly, the scientist is destroyed by his own savage, ancient instincts. Petrol pumps shining a giant 'Save' message into the vast desert twilight speak of an equally uncertain people.[5]

Frank's communication of all of this is held within his choice of composition, the angle of his shot and the time at which it was taken, conspiring to reveal the truth of this moment, a time and place that we would otherwise miss. He is again the visionary, proclaiming what he sees, the artist revealing the signs by which we understand the world, and the prophet, sending back postcards from the wilderness that we might understand.

Notes

1. See Chapter 12 for a fuller examination of the three images discussed here.

2. Guillame Apollinaire described the role of the artist:

> It is the social function of great poets and artists to continually renew the appearance nature has for the eyes of men. Without poets, without artists, men would soon weary of nature's monotony. The sublime idea men have of the universe would collapse with dizzying speed. The order which we find in nature, and which is only an effect of art, would at once vanish. Everything would break up in chaos … Poets and artists plot the characteristics of their epoch, and the future docilely falls in with their desires. (Apollinaire 1949: 14)

3. Margaret Bourke-White also featured a harmonium in her photographs of *Exminster, South Carolina* in *You Have Seen Their Faces*, her collaboration with writer Erskine Caldwell, published in 1937. The instrument here is a mute onlooker, watching the holy-roller activities of the hut-like church's congregation. It is not being played in any of her images; its teeth-like keys face the dais, an object apparently integrated into the action. It is, however, the only externally manufactured fitting in the church, all else being obviously constructed by the faithful. This external, technological feel leaves a slight sense of inappropriateness, of a cold, dead machine in an otherwise very improvised human environment. Bourke-White's theme is the activities of the worshippers. Her repetition of the same interior with different activities signals this, as do her captions. Evans' genius lies in the removal of the faithful, focusing on the object and its significance. Without the easy identification which the presence of other human beings allows, Evans causes us to examine the harmonium as a thing.

4. In its juxtaposition of a small element of culture with a wild landscape, this image echoes Cartier-Bresson's *Mexico* (Cartier-Bresson Foundation/Magnum). The religious significance of 'Save' echoes Cartier-Bresson's cross.

5. The film's futuristic visuals were also influential across the Atlantic. Richard Hamilton, working with John McHale and John Voelker, used a huge blow-up of a scene from the film as part of an installation for the *This is Tomorrow* exhibition at the Whitechapel Gallery in 1956. The scene chosen features 'Robbie', a friendly robot carrying the unconscious heroine to safety. The grip of his glinting metallic mechanoid fingers on her flesh communicates the ambivalence of the part-formed relationships between humanity and its new technology far more directly than anything by Frank does. There are reasons for this. This is an image intended for easy reading. It is also fantasy. Frank was dealing with the signals of this newly exploding relationship as they existed in reality. He also had no desire to be simplistic.

9

The Americans' Response To *The Family of Man* Exhibition

Robert Frank's association with Edward Steichen has already been mentioned. Frank said:

> Steichen liked me a lot and he was very good to me. I just didn't agree with his sentimentality about photographs any more. I had used up the single, beautiful image. I was aware that I was living in a different world—that the world wasn't as good as that—that it was a myth that the sky was blue and that all photographs were beautiful. (Frank, in Johnson 1989: 37)

Steichen mounted the highly influential *The Family of Man* exhibition at the Museum of Modern Art, New York in 1955, the year in which Frank began his *Americans* journey. Frank assisted Steichen with its preparation, and several of his photographs were included. *The Americans*, not surprisingly given the photographers' close association, follows many of the exhibition's themes and echoes many of its images, but in a manner clearly out of sympathy with *The Family of Man*'s philosophy. *The Americans* comments upon, contends with and occasionally subverts Steichen's chosen images.

In the introduction to the exhibition catalogue, Steichen wrote:

> I believe *The Family of Man* exhibition is the most ambitious and challenging project photography has ever attempted. It was conceived as a mirror of the universal elements and emotions in the everydayness of life—as a mirror of the essential oneness of mankind throughout the world. *The Family of Man* has been created in a passionate spirit of devoted love and faith in man. (Steichen 1955: 3)

The Family of Man signally fails as a 'mirror of the universal elements and emotions' because of its refusal to squarely face the truth. Its treatment of the Second World War is symptomatic. The exhibition was mounted ten short years after the horrors of the Holocaust. The exhibition referred to it in a single image. In a picture by an unknown photographer, German soldiers herd Polish Jews out of a burning Warsaw Ghetto (n.d., Archive of the Nürnberg Trials). The soldiers are detestable in their oppression of the weak, yet this is as far as *The Family of Man* would go. The Jews leaving the ghetto are harried yet noble. They march upright. Two young women, a child and an old man lead the column. They reveal nobility in physical weakness, nobility in adversity. Margaret Bourke-White, who is featured elsewhere in the exhibition, took photographs in the Concentration Camps to which these Jews were condemned. These are not included. There is no nobility in the emaciated carcasses of Auschwitz.

Steichen was not stupid. It cannot be assumed that he or his collaborators were unaware of reality. They simply did not want to look at it. The American Dream at its most facile depends on the perfectibility of the human race. In many ways, this is also the central hope of Modernism. The Holocaust was perceived as a terrible and unfortunate mistake, an inexplicable aberration. The atrocities perpetrated previously by the British and the Americans on a variety of indigenous peoples were conveniently forgotten. The world should not be this way. *The Family of Man* orders its photographs in a world as it ought to have been and not as it was. Steichen's 'passionate spirit of devoted love' (1955: 3) finds form in his faith that one day ugliness and injustice will be banished. The implication is that if we ignore evil and darkness, or at most tacitly acknowledge them, then perhaps they will go away. To look at these things seems to be felt to in some way encourage them. The exhibition's success attests to the acceptance of its world-view by its American visitors. With God and the American Way, surely this dream can come to pass.

The reality of the country was very different. America in the fifties was no techno utopia. It was waging a crusade against communism, partially as a response to the explosion of the first Russian nuclear bomb in 1949. Senator Joe McCarthy's *Committee for Anti-American Activities* practiced its inquisition like witch hunts and celebrated their associated *auto da fe*. Political unconformity was effectively outlawed. Frank himself was arrested by Lieutenant Brown of the Little Rock Police because of:

> the man's appearance, the fact that he was a foreigner and had in his possession cameras…we are continually being advised to watch out for any persons illegally in the country in the employ of some unfriendly foreign power and the possibility of Communist affiliations. (Frank, in Tucker and Brookman 1986: 24)

Xenophobia and racism were rife, deeply woven into the texture of the nation. By a significant coincidence, the very same Little Rock in which Frank was arrested would explode into violence three years later, as whites attempted to prevent the racial integration of its Central High School. This would require the army's intervention. Frank felt this: 'Seeing those faces, those people, the kind of hidden violence in the country at that time, the McCarthy period I felt it very strongly.' (Frank, in Janis and MacNeil 1977: 54). The refusal by *The Family of Man*, and by extension America, to embrace the whole truth is part of the impetus to opinion which Frank describes.

Alongside the sense of 'hidden violence', Frank saw the new material creed of America, in which mass production and the material richness of the land supplied the conditions for the nascent consumerist world. He saw the things of the spirit being commodified and acquiring material equivalents: Television evangelists and others who put God and salvation up for sale were another symptom. This is the society which *The Family of Man* reflected and to which Frank responded.

It would not be satisfactory, however, to see Frank as just an *enfant terrible*, ripping up his former mentor Steichen's take on humanity and culture. He wrote:

> I have often been accused of deliberately twisting subject matter to my point of view... Opinion often consists of a kind of criticism. But criticism can come out of love. (Frank, in Maloney 1958: 115)

His critique, he claims, was from a perspective of love. This, though, is a love that, unlike Steichen's, acknowledges the importance of honesty.

Frank's close knowledge of *The Family of Man* is unsurprising given his involvement in its creation. *The Americans*' photographs often closely respond to particular images from Steichen's show. Frank sought the sometimes prosaic, sometimes challenging reality behind the exhibition's toothy smile.

The Family of Man included over twenty images of a mother and child. All of these were racially matched. Two images especially represent the USA, one by Irving Penn from *Vogue* (collection of *Vogue*) and the other by Nell Dorr (Museum of Modern Art, New York). The first is an image of sophistication, the second of warm homeliness. Frank's photograph *Charleston, South Carolina* shows a smiling black nanny and her tiny white charge. They are clearly happy together. The implications are obvious. Here is a relationship that transcends race. The expression on the baby's face makes such issues ridiculous. Kerouac wrote his introduction around the same time as the inter-racial violence in Arkansas mentioned above was happening. He said of this picture:

> ...the sweet little white baby in the black nurse's arms both of them bemused in heaven, a picture that should have been hanged in Little Rock showing love under the sky and in the womb of our universe the Mother. (Kerouac, in Frank 1959: 6)

Frank further challenges *The Family of Man*'s depiction of American motherhood. The woman in Irving Penn's picture looks as though she might be the employer of just such a nanny. This black woman is *in loco maternis*, more real to this child than her remote natural mother. Nell Dorr's picture of a blissful, nightgowned, breastfeeding mother is white on white on white. The bond between the white baby and a black breast is eschewed by Steichen, but eloquently addressed by Frank.

Frank similarly challenges *The Family of Man*'s consideration of lovers. Steichen used a photograph originally published in *Life* magazine by Ralph Morse (collection of *Life*), and another by Edward Weston (Museum of Modern Art, New York), in which happy lovers embrace, apparently oblivious to the camera or the world beyond themselves. Frank's *San Francisco* also figures a couple lying in an embrace. They are black, and stare challengingly out of the image, clearly discomfited by the photographer's presence. There is no possibility here of *The Family of Man*'s suspension of disbelief. This photograph is revealed as the product of a particular process, with intrusive and voyeuristic overtones. Frank's lovers are disturbed by him and, through guilt by association, his viewers. The oblivious lovers of Morse's image and the consenting ones of Weston's serve the fiction of the photograph as impartial observation. They equally serve the fiction of loving as a universal panacea. Frank's subjects, who moments before were lying together on the grass, are in an instant ready for conflict.

Steichen features many photographs of men and women working. Included in these are images of sweat and toil in dusty, dirty conditions. A Bolivian woman breastfeeds her baby in a quarry with a shovel at her feet (G. Thorlichen, Museum of Modern Art, New York). A black man stands between resignation and despair inside a stone-crushing plant (D. Kessel, Museum of Modern Art, New York). A Welsh child with a bandaged finger holds his miner's lamp, dirty in the pit (F. Scherschel, collection of *Life*). These photographs are accompanied by the text 'If I didn't work these worlds would perish'. The caption is taken from *The Bhagavad Gita*, an Indian religious text credited as the dictation of the incarnated Krishna. What relevance do the words of an Indian deity speaking of his divine activities have in this context? Is Steichen equating these workers with God? Or is anything acceptable, so long as it serves the exhibition's purpose? In any case, the exhibition's implication is clear. All of this, however squalid or painful, is necessary and desirable. Steichen hammers his point home further. A Russell Lee photograph, originally taken for the Farm Security Administration, shows the crippled arthritic hands of a woman (collection of the Library of Congress). This sits above the caption 'Bless thee in all the work of thy hand which thou doest' taken from Deuteronomy 14:29 in the Bible. Karl Marx's description of religion as the opiate of the masses (Marx 1977: 127) could not be better illustrated than here. The implication is that a life of crippling work is God's will, and these useless hands that are its fruit should be worn like a trophy.

One of Steichen's worker images is a Bill Brandt picture of a young dark-haired woman, taken from *A Camera in London* (*East End Morning*, B. Brandt, 1948, estate of

B. Brandt). She is scrubbing the tiled floor of a hallway, with the door open, allowing the viewer to see her. Her body describes a beautiful arabesque as she wets her brush or cloth in a bucket. She looks down and to the right, in a traditional Madonna-like pose. She seems perhaps wistful, perhaps a little sad, a delicate female at her work.[1]

Frank's *Elevator Miami Beach* features another brown-haired girl. She is uniformed and at the controls of the cited elevator. The dark form of a bald man blurs across the photograph's right. To the left, a woman in a white fur stole is similarly blurred. The operator herself is static within this movement and looks at neither of them. Her expression almost defies description. It contains the longing for something more, hatred of the tyranny of the time spent endlessly riding this elevator, delivering faceless people who she doesn't see, doesn't especially care about and who similarly neither see nor care for her. Her uplifted eyes appear to see nothing; she has retreated into herself, waiting for her life to recommence. Yet she is not cowed. She is defiant. Her impatience is burned across her face. She wants to live, though she has to endure this work. There is nothing of the Madonna here, no wistful long-suffering. Here is a flesh and blood woman, working because she has to. No amount of captioning or religious quotations will change her essential nature, revealed in this 'look of sadness' (Frank, in Maloney 1958: 115). Kerouac said in his introduction, 'That little ole lonely elevator girl looking up sighing in an elevator full of blurred demons, what's her name & address?' (Kerouac, in Frank 1959: 6). Frank does not depict an archetype or a cipher, or attempt to generalize or universalize working. His woman at work is real enough to arouse Kerouac. This typifies Frank's examination of people working in America, as we will see in Part Three of our consideration.

Frank in *The Americans* is looking for the honest truth of his subjects, insofar as a photograph can deliver it. His pictures do 'mirror … the universal elements and emotions in the everydayness of life' to an extent, as Steichen described his intentions for his show. Yet Frank's work, and photography in general, cannot effectively act as a 'mirror of the essential oneness of mankind throughout the world' (Steichen 1955: 3) if that oneness doesn't exist. Photography cannot wish it into being. Even the subverting and diverting texts of Steichen's exhibition do not successfully smudge the reality beneath. As Frank said, 'The world wasn't as good as that.' (Frank, in Johnson 1989: 37).

Note

1. Walker Evans, as in so many cases, provides us with a precedent for this picture. His *New Orleans* (1935, estate of Walker Evans) shows a young black woman leaning indolently against a wooden wall, looking with something of the same enigmatic intensity as the elevator operator. Nearer to the viewer, a hatted man walks in front of her in blurred oblivion.

10

The Americans and the Promotional Images of the Standard Oil Company

Robert Frank, in his examination of American civilization, deals with a sophisticated subject in a sophisticated way. He said, 'If the photographer wants to be an artist, his thoughts cannot be developed overnight at the corner drugstore …' (Frank, in Maloney 1958: 115). We have seen that his photograph *U.S. 90, en route to Del Rio, Texas* functions as a revelation of the author to his audience, but, at the same time, it comments on a classic Standard Oil advertising image. Sol Libsohn's *Charles Kitchen, Anchor Motor Freight Company trucker, driving at night on U.S. Highway 22; May, 1945* (Standard Oil Archive, University of Louisville) was part of a project called *Truck Story*, on which he worked from March until May of 1945. Libsohn and Roy Stryker, Standard Oil's Picture File Director, together produced a script detailing a routine two-day journey by two truckers collecting parts for warplanes. The story was published in *The Lamp*, Standard Oil's expensively produced corporate magazine, with *Charles Kitchen* as its lead image. The magazine was circulated to politicians, stockholders, publishers and the like.

Frank's *U.S. 90, en route to Del Rio, Texas* follows the composition of Libsohn's image closely. The line of both vehicles is approximately a fifth of the way in from the edge. The position of the windscreens and the view through them of people inside, are very similar. Most significant of all are the lit headlamps, occupying about the same position in each picture. Notably, Frank has reversed the Standard Oil composition, literally mirroring it, as his photograph mirrors, distorts and comments on its meaning.

Libsohn's almost cinematic image presents the trucker as an archetypal worker-hero. Humphrey Bogart had previously played exactly such a trucker, in Henri-Georges Clouzot's *The Wages of Fear* (1952), heroically carrying nitroglycerine across rugged country in an effort to preserve life and limb. Kerouac acknowledged this archetype:

> ...what a driver a great big tough truck driver with popping eyes and a hoarse raspy voice who just slammed and kicked at everything and got his rig under way and paid hardly any attention to me. (Kerouac 1972: 16)

If the American Dream presses the road and the notion of journey into service as signifiers of a better life waiting just around the corner, then images such as Charles Kitchen identify the pursuers of this dream as heroes rather than victims. Advertising is mythologizing the worker. It is the aesthetic humanization of industry, the justification of hours of toil by the conferral of heroic status. *Charles Kitchen* is a corporate image, full of machismo and power. The photograph's low viewpoint emphasizes the truck's size; its lines are rectilinear and powerful. The glowing, eyelike headlamp sits above and to the side of the toothy radiator grill, grinning against the black bonnet. Charles' face is determined, lit dramatically from the side. His grip on the steering wheel is certain. Libsohn wrote, 'His hands were big on the wheel. They seemed hardly to try when he turned the wheel' (Libsohn, in Keller 1986: 204). He is the master of this monster, controlling its huge power, driving through the night with his war-bound cargo, intent on his mission. He embodies not only the nobility of labour and of Standard Oil, but of America, intent on the defeat of the enemies of the 'free world'.

In contrast, Frank's image is taken from head height. This emphasises normality, facilitating an easy identification with the photograph's everydayness. The car is small and personal; its curves are feminine and humble. Frank's Madonna-like wife and child sleep easily. The car stands motionless at the side of a desert road in dim light. There is no urgency, no work to do, nowhere to go that can't wait. The only imperatives are personal. The only mission is the journey, the only cargo his family. Here, Frank has entirely subverted the notion of the highway as the conduit for affairs of state. Charles Kitchen is a cog in the wheel of the Dream, aiding the American pursuit of 'manifest destiny', in this case by helping to win a war. He is a part of the industrial process; both he and the road are its servants. Frank's road is a private place, somewhere to watch his family sleep, somewhere that is as close as this wild-at-heart world comes to home. The road is the conduit of his personal journey, perhaps even of his dreams. He denies its role in the formulas of advertising men, and through it questions the orthodoxy of the American Dream. The road is revealed as an aspect of the wide world through which it runs, a world bigger than society's strictures, a strange, mysterious and wonderful place. Frank's photograph is an image of living, his existence and journey described by a family and a car, their travel through time and space described by the road and the desert.

Charles Kitchen is personally unimportant. He stands for faceless millions in his photograph. Another driver would have done just as well, without Libsohn even having to change the story. Charles is a representative member of society, his individuality serving the whole. Frank's photograph reveals an individual following his own obscure purposes.

Frank in *The Americans* appears to respond to images from the Standard Oil Picture File on many occasions. The visual similarities between its images and his own strongly argue intent. Given his clear and stated reaction to that other visual representation of America, *The Family of Man* exhibition, this is not surprising. There were plenty of opportunities for Frank to see images from Standard Oil's File. It served the company's public relations department, which was charged with providing publicity images wherever and whenever they were wanted. The File's images were exploited extensively. The Civil Affairs Division of the US Army, for example, used them to illustrate 'the American Way of Life to People Overseas' (Stryker 1947). They featured in *Life, Look* and the *Saturday Evening Post,* among other magazines and newspapers. In 1949 alone, 667 Standard Oil File pictures were carried by the press. Textbooks and encyclopaedias also used the photographs. Another popular means of dissemination was panel-mounted display sequences. The Picture File produced 264 differently themed arrangements of photographs. In 1949 around 10,000 of these were needed to satisfy demand (Keller 1986: 47). Many galleries also featured Standard Oil's images. Harvard University and the Franklin Institute in Philadelphia both hosted an exhibition called *The Architecture of Oil.* The Museum of Modern Art in New York featured the work of four Standard Oil photographers in its *In and Out of Focus: A Survey of Today's Photography* exhibition (Museum of Modern Art exhibition number 373, 6 April—11 July 1948). Steichen's *Family of Man* show included an image from the file, which showed children dancing in a circle outside a school in Peru, sited beneath an oil derrick. This again reveals the extent to which these images were known.

Trolley – New Orleans is another of Frank's photographs which echo Standard Oil's imagery. In 1947, Esther Bubley took a series of photographs illustrating a cross-country bus journey. This would appear two years later, in volume 31 of *The Lamp*, as 'Via Bus' and in *Photo Memo,* a smaller, specialized magazine advertising the Picture File's latest photographs, under the title 'By Bus'. Bubley photographed *Greyhound Bus Terminal, N.Y.C. Loaded bus ready to depart* (Standard Oil Archive, University of Louisville) in July of that year. Three side windows of a Greyhound fill the top half of the image. These are illuminated, the interior warm and busy against the darker tone of the bus's side. The affluent white passengers are furred and hatted: some smile, some are glum. Crisp, white-covered seats leave no doubt that every effort has been made to ensure their comfort. A legend painted along the coach reads 'Coast to Coast'. These travellers are, after all, the descendants of the pioneers; they also journey the wide land.

Frank's image is entirely other. Five windows similarly occupy the top half of the photograph, but the passengers thus framed are very different to Bubley's. White faces occupy the windows to the left. The first is evanescent behind the glass. The second passenger stares with unveiled suspicion and distaste at the photographer and, through him, by implication at the viewer. Black hair and a dark coat frame her disdain, an expression as evil as the witch in MGM's hugely popular 1939 version of *The Wizard of Oz*. Behind her, a white boy and his sister have a caged look, the boy clinging to the bar-like window frame. His hair, suit and bowtie define him as middle class and middle management in embryo. This boy stands in stark contrast to the dearly loved dream of adventurous and anarchic American boyhood, described in *Tom Sawyer* and *Huckleberry Finn* (Twain, 1876 and 1884). This is boyhood at its most suppressed, exactly 'the look of sadness' (Frank, in Maloney 1958: 115) that Frank sought. The matronly perpetrator of this bondage broods protectively in the shadows.

To the right, towards the back of the bus, sit two black people. They have no option but to sit here; the photograph was taken before the US Congress ruled that segregated buses were unconstitutional, on 20 December 1956. The black man is powerfully built. He echoes the white boy's position, yet his open-shirted body language speaks an appeal. He appears to be in supplication. The white boy looks trapped, but at the same time holds himself with a confidence entirely lacking from the muscular adult behind. Not all of these colour-classified and restricted passengers seem uneasy with their demarcation. The black lady at extreme right seems to be staring unconcernedly out of shot.

Frank's image is uncomfortable. It examines racism in America without overtly representing it. The photograph's tension exists in the unequal appearance and body language of its subjects. Its message is heightened enormously by its position, following *Fourth of July—Jay, New York*, a photograph of white families comfortably celebrating Independence Day beneath the Red, White and Blue supposed signifier of the equality of all men. Perhaps most significantly of all, the tension lies in the hindsight-equipped eye of the viewer. We are all, I suspect, looking for the unassuming Rosa Parks, quietly and unwittingly starting a revolution by refusing to give up her seat.

Frank, then, has taken Bubley's representative American image and rewritten it. His observation of the faces in *Trolley Bus* reveals the reality of an America far more complex and divided than Standard Oil would dare depict.

Frank's deconstruction of the work of Standard Oil, conscious or otherwise, is not limited to particular responses to individual images. The Picture File was a major contributor to the developing iconography of America, and notably of the American diner. Jovial Americans consuming quantities of food are frequently represented and celebrated. This is not surprising. By advertising its ability to feed its population (occasionally to the point of obesity), America contrasts itself starkly with the shortages and rationing experienced throughout Europe. Eating is one of our most basic needs. In primitive societies, body weight was a sign of beauty. The Venus of Willendorf (c. 24,000–22,000 BCE, Naturhistorisches Museum, Vienna), a 20,000-year-old sculpture from central Europe, is of an obese woman. This has an understandable physiological basis. Women need to achieve a certain body weight in order to be fertile. In times of famine, they lose the ability to conceive children. The lamentable but widespread notion of the 'ideal' female figure has repeatedly shifted through time, often reflecting times of plenty and of difficulty, and echoing the associated shifts of visual-cultural fashions. Thus the popularity in the 1940s and '50s of full-figured actresses like Jayne Mansfield and Jayne Russell was a reaction to the privations and starvation of the Second World War, celebrating well-fed American womanhood. The affluent, and for a while at least optimistic, 1960s were unafraid of food shortages and saw a swing to waif-like gamines, the models 'Twiggy' and Jean Shrimpton being examples. The relationship between visual-cultural fashion and the shape of women is usefully demonstrated in the bulbous bosses, finials and adornments of American cars of the post-war years, reflecting the fascination with the full breast. English artist Richard Hamilton comments amusingly on this in his *Hommage a Chrysler Corp* (1957, Tate Gallery), in which he directly connects the front bumper of a Chrysler car to the body part that inspired it, and which, through its placing as well as its shape, it represents.

The American diner represented in Standard Oil's promotional photographs is a microcosm of the land of plenty, peopled by well-fed, fertile women and well-fed, hard-working men who coexist in a happy and harmonious society. Smiling waitresses happily serve customers who are happy to be served. Sol Libsohn's *Truck Story,* which we have already mentioned, exemplifies this. *Group of truckers in Eagle Grill, Akron, Ohio; May 1945* (Standard Oil Archive, University of Louisville) pictures Charles Henry and his associates drinking beer and coffee beneath a neon eagle. They sit in front of a door marked 'men'. A buxom young waitress serves them the latest in what appears to be a long line of drinks. She is smiling winningly at them, perhaps sharing a joke. The message is clear. This is the place for the men who serve the eagle. Happiness and fulfilment, materially and socially, follow as a natural consequence of working for the nation. There is even an intimation of sexual promise. It may be limited to flirting, but for these crabbed drivers that pleasure may not be an inconsiderable one. The young waitress certainly accepts them and appears to enjoy her role and their company. Uncle Sam and his aquiline familiar are looking after their own.

Jack Kerouac was not blind to the diner's charms. He too celebrated the almost ritual intake of copious amounts of comestibles, in the party atmosphere of the eating-place. He wrote:

> We stopped along the road for a bite to eat. The cowboy went off to have a spare tire patched and Eddie and I sat down in a kind of homemade diner. I heard a great laugh, the greatest laugh in the world, and here came this rawhide old timer Nebraska farmer with a bunch of other boys into the diner; you could hear his raspy cries clear across the plains, across the whole gray world of them that day. Everybody else laughed with him. He didn't have a care in the world. (Kerouac, 1972: 19)

This is, of course, not surprising or anomalous. So many of the photographs that image the American diner echo Kerouac's experience. There is no doubt that many of these suggestions of a land of plenty and a happy society in which everyone, especially the stranger, is welcomed were reasonably accurate and ingenuous. Frank had, after all, contributed to this visual strophe with a 'happy diner' picture of his own, one of his contributions to *The Family of Man*. He recorded several jovial young women laughing and eating beneath a huge 'Hamburger' sign in New York. Although their hairstyles and clothes are almost too similar, revealing a worrying degree of social conformity, there is little else that is critical, and Frank's image sits comfortably amongst a number of depictions of people eating, drawn from cultures across the planet. Interestingly, he took a companion photograph at the same time, called *NYC, 14th Street, White Tower Hamburgers* (1948, Museum of Modern Art, New York). This shows the same women looking out of their window with caution and a little aggression. It is not surprising that Steichen took the image he did.

In *The Americans*, however, Frank's reactions to the figurations of the diner in the images of Standard Oil and others is typically considered and sophisticated. The nearest he ever comes to Kerouac's bonhomie is in *En route from New York to Washington, Club Car.* The train's dining car is lit with fluorescent light. Half of the photograph is occupied by the backs of two tweed-jacketed men. They are hunched conspiratorially, blocking us out. The camera is at chair level, looking up, a viewpoint that heightens the sense of exclusion. Between the jackets is a bald man's head. He listens to the left-hand jacket, ignoring the camera utterly. Our isolation in this transient, stark environment is complete. The jovial inclusivity of Kerouac's Nebraska, or of the *Eagle Grill* is entirely absent here.

This exclusion and isolation of the stranger is repeated in *Bar – Gallup, New Mexico.* Again, the brilliant coldness of fluorescent light bathes the photograph. The camera seems to be at knee height and the unusual angle of the composition suggests a photograph shot off without using the viewfinder, taken surreptitiously. The only person entirely in view is a cowboy-hatted man. He stands, relaxed yet confrontational, facing a group of figures whose black bulk occupies the right-hand third of the photograph. The image is redolent of cinematic images of gunfights and Old West saloons, places of threat and fear rather than of welcome and bonhomie. This dark, foreboding place brings to mind Frank's experience 'another time, in the South':

> …a fellow turned up wearing a big hat. Same question. I say 'I'm looking, I'm travelling around'. He takes a big watch out of his pocket and says to me 'I'm the sheriff, you have one hour to leave town'. We think that only happens in films. (Frank 1991: 63)

The isolation of the traveller, even in the diner, the symbol of American hospitality is again explored in *Restaurant – U.S. 1 leaving Columbia, South Carolina.* This is a multi-faceted image, discussing religion, as we have seen, in addition to isolation. For now, we may see it as a room, with a table, chairs, condiments and an ashtray, which is empty of people. The only company is a switched-on TV: people are replaced by a machine with a picture of a person. There is no flesh and blood, so a simulacrum must suffice. A suited man on the screen is engaged in a transaction with someone or something out of shot. In the moment that Frank pressed his shutter, even this electronic companion is ignoring his viewers. The human, contained world of this four-square diner is infiltrated and compromised by a brilliant flood of daylight burning through the window. Its radiance covers the table and a chair. Its brilliance outshines the man made light of the TV tube, spreading itself across the room. It is redolent of the bright morning outside, the natural world, the world beyond society. Kerouac, in his introduction to Frank's book, called it a 'holy halo I never thought could be captured on film much less described in its beautiful visual entirety in words' (Kerouac, in Frank 1959: 1).

Frank continues his examination of Americans eating in *Cafeteria – San Francisco.* This echoes another image from Standard Oil's *Truckers Story*, Libsohn's *Charles Henry eating steak at Martin's restaurant, Darlington, Pa.; March 1945* (Standard Oil Archive, University of Louisville). Charles sits squeezed into a suit, shirt and tie. His clothes look as though they will burst at any moment, as he resolutely cuts into a plate-sized steak, lips parted in anticipation. His hands are corpulent, wearing a large, square ring. The dark tones of the photograph suggest warmth and safety. The child at top left who looks with apparent longing at Charles' dinner, strikes a slightly jarring note, an unintentional one, I suspect.

Frank's photograph follows Libsohn's composition quite closely. *San Francisco* pictures a man sitting in about the same position as Charles, also eating steak. His table is squalid, though, covered in the remains of other people's meals. The man's clothes are not as smart as Charles', although neither are they threadbare. The room doesn't have the protective darkness of 'Martin's Diner'; it is well lit. The back of a hat and coated man suggests a busy and impersonal place. Perhaps the most defining characteristic of Frank's picture is the expression on its subject's face. It is exactly that 'look of sadness' (Frank, in Maloney 1958: 115) of which Frank wrote. He may be eating steak, his clothes may be reasonable but this is a despondent image of a man for whom no amount of cafeteria food will bring joy or inclusion. He takes little delight in the meal; his mind on other things. He is an individual who sits in this American institution untouched by its mythology; its disorder and sense of alienation emphasize his absorption in his own experiences.

Charity ball - New York City precedes the man in the San Franciscan Cafeteria and reinforces its loneliness. There, a woman in shining jewellery and an evening gown accepts a kiss from a man. She appears content, gently touching his hand while her other hand cradles a cigarette. On the well-ordered table in front of them a lamp burns, illuminating the woman's expression. These two photographs contrast conditions of wealth, certainly, but more than that they contrast a deep sense of contentment and satisfaction with despondency. One of these photographs pictures people in relationship, the other a man who is signally alone. The diner does nothing to alleviate his evident suffering.

Drug store – Detroit further comments on the bonhomie of images like Esther Bubley's *Greyhound Bus depot, Scranton, Pa. Bus passengers eating lunch at the terminal lunch counter; September 1947* (Standard Oil Archive, University of Louisville), another of her *Bus Story* photographs. Bubley's photograph looks over a busy but tidy counter. Steel cups with protruding straws suggest milkshakes. A man at extreme right ladles soup into himself. The eye height viewpoint suggests normality and comfort. The viewer sees the room as it would be if one was there. The lighting is also comfortable, neither too bright nor too dim. A woman's face is at the exact centre of the composition. She is smiling, engaged in intercourse of some kind with someone out of shot to the right. Her manicured hand holds her straw in readiness. The pleasure of consumption is delayed momentarily for the pleasure of fun with her companions. Another woman to her right watches her with satisfaction; she has an approving and friendly audience. Both wear light, clean blouses. Their hair is neat and attractive. An older man to the left is shirt-and-tie dignified. He doesn't hassle them, content with his lunch; he is turned instead towards a larger female, perhaps his wife. The image is of order. Everything is very proper, yet fun. No one is tired, no one is sweating. This is diner Utopia again.

Frank leads us quietly to the side of this staged idealization and directs us to a view, through a window, on to other, mostly unself-conscious diners in his *Drug store – Detroit*. Nothing is really amiss with the diner: it isn't dirty or squalid. The harsh contrast with Bubley's *Scranton* lies in the faces of its customers. None of them are smiling; they look bored, dissolute and uncomfortable. Two of them look with suspicion at Frank as he photographs them. It is the kind of suspicion that might erupt into disapproval, even threat. One baseball-capped customer covers his mouth protectively with his hand. He stares into space, oblivious of his companions. The sloping diner counter leads the eye across and down to a black-haired man at far right. This leading of the eye echoes *Parade – Hoboken*, which similarly focuses on a face at the right. The man here hunches over his milkshake in a primal gesture of protection, like a predator over its kill. He has an aggressive look, the kind that demands space, demands that it is not disturbed. None of the customers is engaged in any interaction with the others. There is no community here, only a group of disparate and dissociated individuals, who nonetheless sit closely together in a temporary truce, regimented before the counter. Frank's composition expresses this tension. Bubley used a frontal composition, which suggests space, while Frank shoots obliquely along the counter from its corner, foreshortening its sweep and compressing the space occupied by each of the diners, revealing and heightening their mutual isolation. This claustrophobia is heightened as their personal and pictorial space is further invaded by huge cardboard glasses of Orange Whip (at 10 c. each, King Size 15 c.). Other assorted signs hang from the ceiling.[1]

Frank's *Ranch Market – Hollywood* is another assault on American gastric *bonhomie*. In the photograph, a counter assistant glowers, staring out of shot, ignoring Frank and his camera. Her eyes are coldly half-closed, her lipsticked mouth pursed. Above her hang several signs. They proclaim the lack of filler in the market's burgers and their range of products and prices. The central sign is a maniacal Santa Claus with an alcoholic's red cheeks, proclaiming 'Merry Christmas' in a Gothic script. The lines of the ceiling and shelving converge slightly towards the left. This subtle view, neither fully sidelong nor fully frontal, revealing only the head of the waitress, is unfamiliar and uncomfortable. Is she irritated by a customer, perhaps, or bored by the tedium of countless burgers and shakes? She has no Christmas spirit, merely standing behind her counter, defying the drudgery, defying the customers. She certainly has no smile for the men of the eagle. There is no suggestion of flirtatious willingness, no happy cafe society welcoming every passing driver. The demented Santa and this dour waitress stand against Libsohn's eagle and *ingénue* in Frank's unflattering revelation. It is not the whole truth, but it is an important part of it, part that needs acknowledgement. Frank here figures that part of the inconvenient truth which Standard Oil and others chose to ignore.

There are other aspects of Standard Oil's output which are significant for our consideration of *The Americans*. Frank's *View from hotel window - Butte, Montana* interestingly critiques John Collier's *Crested Butte, coal mining town* taken for Standard Oil in 1948 (Standard Oil archive, University of Louisville). Collier's image looks along a sunlit high street at a small collection of buildings. Behind them, verdant hills rise into a wispy-clouded sky. A silhouetted bell tower points the viewer heavenwards, to the glory of summer. There is no evidence whatsoever of mining, despite the title. The road is a dirt track and the buildings are made of planks and corrugated steel, but there are no winding houses or slag tips in sight.

Frank's view from his hotel window pans out from Collier's. Taken from a high window, it is framed by dirty net curtains. These create a misty impression, echoing the smoke escaping from the engine house and the smog of this coal fired, wintry city. Frank has photographed Butte in shadow on a dull day, the flat light exposing this miserable aspect of the functional, jerry-built town. The gray day is an analogue to the factories, flat industrial roofs and derelict land. Frank's high vantage point reveals the coal heaps, winding gear and slag tips, which are hidden behind the painted street fronts of Collier's town.[2] Frank's image is less pretty than Collier's, but reveals far more. In the face of this degree of window dressing, Frank is figuring the dreariness of this world, so successfully ignored by Collier.

Frank, in his response to images from Standard Oil's Picture File, seeks to see beyond the polemic to the actuality of the world before him. He examines the smile of Uncle Sam, pictured on the faces and landscape of America and finds 'what is invisible to others—the look of hope or the look of sadness' (Frank, in Maloney 1958: 115). As Frank had planned in his Guggenheim application, he found and recorded:

> The material is there; the practice will be in the photographer's hand, the vision in his mind. I speak of the things that are there, anywhere and everywhere—easily found, not easily selected and interpreted. (Frank 1954, in Greenough 2009: 362)

Notes

1. George Stock in *The Family of Man* (Steichen 1955: 110) used a very similar composition. Beneath the caption 'And the people sat down to eat and to drink, and rose up to play' from Exodus 32: 6, Stock records a lively bar, filled with smiles and dominated by a young couple at the right.

2. Collier had a penchant for sunshine. *The Oil Town of Rangely, Colorado; November, 1948* again sets the four-square functional architecture, truck parks, derricks and derelict land against a huge summer sky. The foreground even features a young woman walking two white dogs, in case the viewer might miss the bonhomie of the place.

11

The Primacy of the Visual

Frank claimed many things for *The Americans*. He was 'trying to give an opinion … of America' (Frank, in Tucker and Brookman 1986: 28), to 'see freshly' and to 'speak of the things that are there—easily found, not easily interpreted' (Frank 1954, in Greenough 2009: 362). He said: 'This project is essentially the visual study of a civilization … carrying its own visual impact without much word explanation' (Frank, in Greenough 2009: 362). These words help us to see his purpose; they iterate and enumerate his intentions. They are not, of course, to be found anywhere in *The Americans*. Instead, Frank chose to visually communicate his purpose and wordlessly reach his conclusions.

Barber shop through screen door – McClellanville, South Carolina communicates Frank's intentions perhaps better than any other image in the book. The mesh of a screen door mirrors the street across from the shop and creates a reflection. The mesh is a distorting mirror, however, its images materially altered from their corresponding reality. Frank's head and shoulders are also partially reflected, but within his head the shadow is deep enough to allow a glimpse of the barber shop inside. Bottles of hair oil and a white, high-backed chair are revealed. The image is literally inside Frank's head. He wrote afterwards:

> With these photographs, I have attempted to show a cross-section of the American population. My effort was to express it simply and without confusion. The view is personal… (Frank, in Maloney 1958: 115)

Frank's effort was to express his personal view simply. *Barber shop through screen door* is literally America through his head and camera, an outsider looking in.

We have noted the enormous importance of Walker Evans and his photographs as models for Frank's efforts.[1] Walker Evans' *Barbershop Havana* is Frank's precedent. The older photographer also recorded barbers' chairs and bottles of hair oil. He also captured his own reflection in the shop's mirror. His image is partially replicated by Frank, in the manner of an *hommage*. Despite being clearly informed by what has gone before, however, Frank's view is distinctly personal, idiosyncratic and new. The shop, with its chairs and bottles, has much more weight in Evans' image, his head being almost an afterthought, presented with a wry smile by the photographer. *Barber shop through screen door* could not exist without the looming, dominating presence of the photographer. All we could see without his shadow would be the distorted reflections of an American suburban street. This, then, is a very real and honest description of the photographer's work, without which we would have none of these potent and totemic memorials of an America most of us could never otherwise see.

If we accept *Barber shop* as a kind of 'thesis statement' from Frank, if Frank is indeed communicating his intentions pictorially, then we should also be able to find a pictorial conclusion. Surprisingly, given his immense efforts to avoid the predictable or expected, this exists as the book's final photograph.

We have discussed *U.S. 90, en route to Del Rio, Texas* already. It is a revelation of the author and at the same time a reaction to an established advertising image. It has, though, another suggestion. The earlier *U.S. 285* was a picture of an empty, bright road running through darkness, an image of searching. In that image's distance is the elusive light, promising glory, its reality unknown, its nature obscure. The photograph suggests a driver's take through the windscreen of a car.

In *U.S. 90*, the artist has stopped and is out of the car, turning back towards it. This is Frank's conclusion: there is no ephemeral bright destination. After two years on the road, he knows Del Rio will be another Main Street, another diner. The journey's end is this realization. There is only now, only this moment, washed up on some dusty roadside. All that remains is those we love, who share our journey, at the dawning of a new day.

Intriguingly, the 1993 Scalo edition of *The Americans* saw Frank add a series of three images to the end *of the book*. Although these were removed from the recent Steidl imprint, they are nonetheless revealing. They emphasize and extend the content of *U.S. 90*. The images are presented in an entirely different format to the rest of the book. Instead of a single photograph, the images are joined together, suggesting a contact sheet. Two of these are alternate takes on *U.S. 90*, Frank presenting his family in their Ford Business Coupe from several angles. The third photograph of the triptych is a truck park. In the final photograph of this final sequence, a pickup to the left and a lorry to the right frame a large sign reading 'Truck Rates'. Behind this is a smaller sign, advertising Coca-Cola above an arrow. The blandness of the dirt park melds through low hills and low buildings into a bland sky. This is the unremarkable immensity of America, a place whose advertisements are more prominent than its products, whose signs seem to dominate its reality.

Frank reminds his viewers again of Standard Oil's advertisements and the arrow recalls his *Los Angeles*. This earlier *Americans* image is a portrait of a dismal street on a dismal day. It stands against the thousand other city postcard clichés, filled with light and excitement. Frank pictures a lone walker striding purposefully out of the photograph's frame, in the direction of an illuminated arrow. This neon has no accompanying text: it is glowing for no discernible reason and pointing for no apparent purpose. It wonderfully describes a nation still unsure of itself and its direction, while dangerously committed to its headlong pursuit. The smaller, less enigmatic arrow on the Scalo *The Americans*' final page, signals Frank's finally achieved ambivalence. America exists, and Frank, with a half-smile, shrugs and finds a bed.

Along the bottom of this third photograph is handwritten 'Andrea, Mary and Pablo, Texas 1956'. This departure from the book's usual caption format is important. Frank reveals his hand. The photographer claims his photographs. This caption is his signature and his benediction.

Note

1. Generally I've avoided too much focus on Evans, as this has been well and thoroughly done already by others. See especially Tod Papageorge's *Walker Evans and Robert Frank: An Essay on Influence* (1981).

Part Three

The Americans as a Photographic Sequence

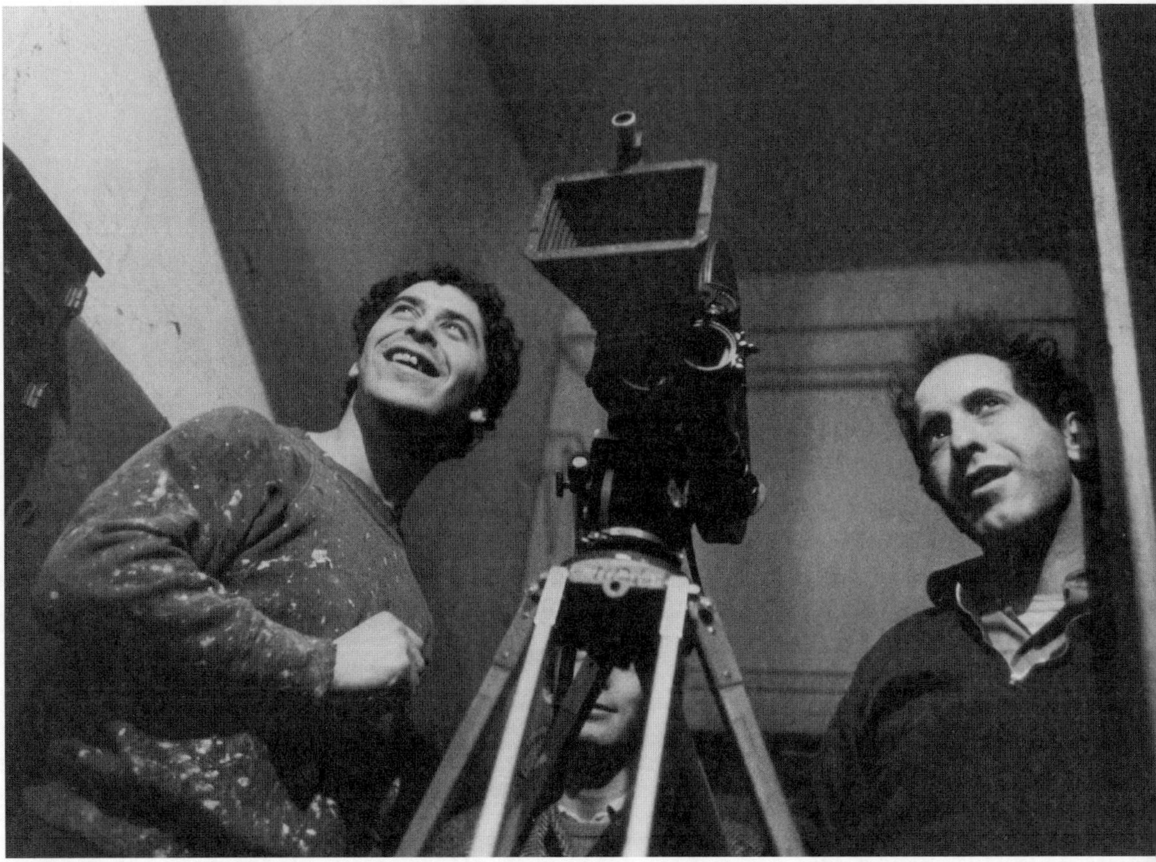

Robert Frank and artist and film director Alfred Leslie, New York, 1959. (Photo by John Cohen/Getty Images)

12

Tracing the Lines of His Hand

Having examined the powerful themes that act architecturally within the book, supporting *The Americans* and stitching it together, we now need to consider the equally important sequential links. Although I am not convinced that Frank's original sectionally structured plan has any real significance for *The Americans* as it was published, I will divide this chapter into four parts for the reader's ease of navigation.

We commented earlier and in detail on the first pair of images (see Chapter 4). They introduce the themes of the significance of the American flag and the comparison of rich and poor, the powerful and powerless. Frank described this as 'the faces of the leaders and the faces of the followers' (Greenough 2009: 362). We have also noted that the first five images are visually linked by the notion of gesture (see Chapter 4). Frank indicated, as we have also examined, that these early images explored the notion of looking and being looked at, the watcher and the watched. We left Frank's procession of images with a cigar-smoking man, two women at his side, watching, according to the caption, a Rodeo.

Typically, as Frank lets go of the notions that have articulated the last several images, he takes up a new theme. These two coexist in *Savannah, Georgia,* a photograph that features another cigar smoker, accompanied by a lady friend, echoing *Rodeo.* This smoker is a soldier, a link that will carry into the following image. The soldier eyes the photographer with suspicion. This is a response that is frequently seen in *The Americans*, reflecting something of the spirit of the times, but also reminding us of the relative novelty, for most people, of being photographed. It serves also to remind us frequently of the eye behind the camera, of the man whose vision this is. The kind of suspicion pictured here reached its apogee for Frank in Little Rock, when a Police Officer locked him in a cell for three days as a suspected Communist.

The active soldier walking along the sidewalk contrasts strongly with another in *Navy Recruiting Station, Post Office – Butte, Montana.* Here, a very static soldier has his feet up on the desk, his indolence heightened ironically by a sign saying: 'Join the Navy, ask me about it.' This image is a significant flag representation and was discussed earlier in Chapter 6.

The stasis and complacency of the recruiting office is contrasted with energy and engagement in *En route from New York to Washington, Club Car.* Here, three men, who are also mature/older, are fully occupied in a discussion. Though not physically active, their body language evidences their activity. There is a strong visual echo: the illuminated stars above the service counter of this train car recall the stars on the flag of the last image. There is also a conceptual link. Although not acknowledged in the title, this train is the 'Congressional Special', an express carrying, at premium cost, businessmen between New York and Washington. The contrast between the idle American Navy recruiting officer and these earnest, engaged American power brokers is effective.

Sarah Greenough, in the excellent 2009 Frank retrospective exhibition catalogue *Looking In*, argues interestingly for a linguistic link with the next image. *Movie Premiere – Hollywood* pictures a glamorously turned out young women, and it is suggested that she might be described as a 'starlet', relating this photograph back to the stars in the train club car. I find this a little doubtful, as there are much stronger visual and conceptual links. The stark contrast between her fresh-faced vitality and the crabbed age of the power brokers balances their interdependence: she is part of the carefully constructed stucco and greasepaint facade that covers and disguises the ruthless capitalism of the Hollywood film industry, one of the industries that the men in the previous image underpin and control. The inclusion of 'Hollywood' in the title is significant, it being both a place and a cipher for a particular and powerful aspect of the American Dream. These images together strongly embody the notion of leaders and followers, which Frank described as a guiding principle in his work.

This glamorous girl instigates a series of photographs focusing on youth. Her aspirations and material well-being, evidenced by her situation and by her fur stole, are contrasted in the next image with more humble, dowdily dressed young people. Frank records these adolescents in a *Candy store – New York City*. The isolation of the Hollywood *ingénue* contrasts with these crowded-together kids, Frank picturing eight people crammed into a small space. The girl at the premiere stands in front of a large Art Deco-styled stucco decoration. This is strongly echoed by the smaller, mass-produced, faux-gilt decoration on the *Candy store*'s jukebox. Jukeboxes are one of the powerful icons of 1950s America that we examined earlier.

The busily interacting group in the candy store is followed by three seated young men in *Motorama – Los Angeles*. Their carefully coiffured hair and the suggestion of white shirt and dark jacket speak affluence, as does their position in the seats of a large new automobile. They are sedate and restrained in their sedan. These carefully presented young men contrast not only with the candy store's denizens but also, markedly, with the next image.

Youth is at the centre again in *New York City*, this time three young men, probably teenagers. They look black and Hispanic. Their sinuous poses, the faux dramatic manner in which one of them looks through his splayed fingers and the partially plucked eyebrows of the boy to the left suggest a degree of gender play, of 'campness'. The time-faded sign behind them, perhaps a playbill, says 'Don't Miss Mister Instin …', I assume it is 'Instinct'. They are engaged fully with the camera, communicating through their eye contact with it, with Frank and thus ultimately with us. This engagement contrasts strongly with the distant and disinterested boys in *Motorama* and the seemingly oblivious youths in *Candy store* and at the premiere.

The next image abandons the emphasis on youth alone and begins a sequence of images concerned with what we might call the 'Ages of Man'. These run from babyhood through to senility, but most often figure parents and children, and contrast youth with age.

Charleston, South Carolina depicts a black nanny with a white baby. This figuration of motherhood, psychological rather than biological, echoes images of the Madonna and child and recalls depictions of Black Sarah, the Gypsy Saint, who was apocryphally the wet nurse of Christ. We considered this image in depth in our discussion of Frank's reaction to *The Family of Man* exhibition.

Ranch Market – Hollywood sees age embodied by a demoniacally grinning Santa, leering down on to a girl counter assistant. She is a picture of stultified boredom: there are signally no lights in her eyes, let alone Christmas cheer. She is a worker, one of a number of images in *The Americans* that examine the world of work and, significantly, critique the representation of this in the 1955 *Family of Man* exhibition, curated by Edward Steichen at the Museum of Modern Art, New York. This show, featuring '503 photographs by 257 photographers from 68 countries' (Steichen 1955: 5), was the zenith of so-called 'humanistic' photography. Its obfuscations and literary diversions gave Frank a board against which to sound, as we have seen.

The market assistant leads us into another image of children in a car, harking back to *Motorama* and forming part of Frank's extensive and detailed critique of the nature and role of the car in American civilization. This small, light-coloured car contrasts with the bourgeois vehicle of the earlier image. The woman, probably a mother, and the two children in *Butte, Montana* are obviously intimate, and this too contrasts with the colder formality of the earlier image. The image of Butte is workaday, the car's rear full of food, the fruits, one assumes, of an earlier shopping expedition. The portly mother, poured into the front seat, is dressed in a plaid shirt and patterned apron, and watches, together with her daughter, something out of shot to the left.

Although these last several images are part of a thematically linked sequence, *Butte, Montana* pairs even more closely with the next image, *Yom Kippur – East River, New York City*. The little family in the car is followed by a photograph of a group of Jewish men and a boy, beside a river. The image is divided along its vertical median line, with the gray-suited 'father', the boy dressed in lightly coloured clothes and the gray river on the right, contrasting with the mostly black left-hand side, occupied by the dark outfits of the Orthodox Jewish men. The boy in this photograph, like the little girl of the last image, is watching something out of frame, this time to the right, the two together thus creating a diptych of sorts. He is in bodily contact with the suited man's back, which might suggest he is a relative. In contrast with the last image, however, in which adult and child look together at the same thing, this adult and child are facing in separate directions, each engaged in his own separate thoughts.

The next photograph is hugely significant for *The Americans*. It marks the beginning of Frank's notional second section. It is part of his consideration of the iconography of the Stars and Stripes and the American Dream, which it embodies. The photograph images a tattered and repaired flag in *Fourth of July – Jay, New York*. It wonderfully embodies Frank's intentions for his book. It describes a collection of adults and children chatting, strolling and milling around, all beneath an overhead Stars and Stripes, which occupies three-fifths of the photograph. Through the flag, the ghost of an American landscape can be seen. Frank has already indicated, through *Parade Hoboken*, that he will describe the people who are covered and subsumed by the flag. Here he is further inviting us to look at the actual people, everyday individuals rather than archetypes or stereotypes, who stand beneath and at the edges of the Star Spangled Banner. This image is part of a very sophisticated series of photographs that we discussed in *People of the Flag* above. All this notwithstanding, the image also continues the theme of adults and children, with the two men at lower right and the boy at lower left clearly echoing the preceding image. Frank, then, uses *Fourth of July—Jay, New York* as a structural device on a number of levels. He uses it as a section marker, while also exploring further the theme of the 'flag', one of the pictorial and thematic groups that stitch the book through. He additionally includes it as one of a sequence of images based around contrasts in age. He thus allows the book to function, and be read, as both a linear and a non-linear presentation.

The next image, *Trolley – New Orleans,* also features a man and a boy, alongside a supporting cast of other adults and children. *Trolley* is one of the more clearly political images within the book, revealing with stark intensity the racial segregation within America during the mid-1950s. The political intentionality of the photograph is difficult to assess. It was taken before the famous 'bus boycott', which bemoaned and eventually caused the outlawing of racially segregated buses. Placing it after the all-white Fourth of July celebrations in Jay, however, clearly juxtaposes the flag, the symbol (albeit everyday, tattered and repaired) of nationhood and the constitution, with clear evidence of oppression and lack of equality. The body position of the young white boy at centre, self-assured in bowtie and jacket, is echoed by that of the hulking black man behind, sitting, as required by law, in the rear of the bus and looking on the world with understandable uncertainty and trepidation. The trolley's windows frame other occupants, as we discussed earlier. Despite their shared space, the framing reveals their intense solitude, loneliness and separation.

Canal Street – New Orleans continues this idea of loneliness. It figures an older man at centre, solitary in a thronging crowd. He is still-seeming within a mass of humanity, most of whom seem intent on navigating the *melee* without acknowledging or engaging with anyone else. The exceptions are familiar. Frank's 'man and boy' motif is repeated again at left, with the man smiling down on the child as if they are sharing some kind of joke. The observant face of a second child at extreme right similarly echoes the expression on the face of a dour and intent older woman. The selection and inclusion of this photograph, with its islands of warmth within a colder, harsher street scene is not surprising, since Frank was a parent, travelling for some of his journey with his family. These almost hidden moments of warmth give the lie to so much of the criticism of *The Americans* at the time of its release. There is a great deal of love and affection within its images. The problem is one of attention and application. Viewers used to the gushing and obvious representations of *The Family of Man* were not, I suspect, used to looking at photographs as one would look at a painting. Nor were they, in many cases, and as Szarkowski observed, prepared to acknowledge that such everyday scenes could contain such profundity:

> The pictures took us by ambush then. We knew the America that they described, of course, but we knew it as one knows the background hum of a record player, not as a fact to recognize and confront. Nor had we understood that this stratum of our experience was a proper concern of artists. (Szarkowski, in Frank 1968: rear cover)

Solitude and age continue into the next image, which this time features a single man standing in the time-darkened, faded porch of *Rooming House – Bunker Hill, Los Angeles.* His face is hidden by the obliquely rising stair, and only his dark-suited body and walking stick are revealed. The architecture is a close analogy for his declined physical condition, both of them having had their glory days and both of them somewhat along the road to ruin. As Shakespeare wonderfully described it in *Othello,* they are 'declined in the vale of years' (2007: 97).

The apparent dissolution and resignation of the old man in *Rooming House* is contrasted with the still-engaged expression of the older man in *Yale Commencement – New Haven Green, New Haven, Connecticut,* continuing the theme of the ages of man. As he watches the stream of younger men walk by, he may appear a little cynical, an expression of world-weary indulgence towards these enthusiastic young things on his face, but his posture, his attire and the newspaper he holds attest to his continued involvement with the world of action. He is separate, but not lost to the world of the others in his photograph.

The next image pictures a baby next to a jukebox, standing incongruously in a timber *Café – Beaufort, South Carolina.* The jukebox appears almost to have landed there like one of the space ships that descended on to a startled earth in so many 1950s science fiction films. Frank recognizes the jukebox as a significant icon of '50s America, as we have seen. The relationship between the jukebox and the black baby is fascinating; it functions perhaps as a 'robot nanny', echoing science fiction again. The form of the machine resembles the much-celebrated robot 'butler' in Fred Wilcox's 1954 blockbuster film *Forbidden Planet.*

The black baby is alone in *Beaufort,* and contrasts with the next photograph, *Georgetown, South Carolina,* which features two women and a child, in a classic pyramidal composition. The composition echoes a number of pyramidally composed Renaissance works depicting the Madonna and Christ. Leonardo da Vinci's *The Virgin and Child with St Anne and St John the Baptist* (National Gallery, London, 1499-1500) is an intriguing comparison. Instead of St Anne's enigmatic finger, pointing towards heaven, the woman in Frank's rendering points upwards with a cigarette. The implication is obvious: there is nothing less significant or important about these women and children in contemporary America. They too are Madonnas and Saint Annes and the anonymous toddler with them is every bit as significant for the contemporary American world as the Christ child or the Baptist. These unknown women are the 'everymen' in whose arcane ways the hope of the redundant world resides. The bankrupt culture of Europe, caught in a spiral of ever more devastating wars, and of which da Vinci and his contemporaries became pillars, must recognize and celebrate this moment of tenderness in Georgetown, or perish. This toddler in matronly company follows the lonely baby in the café in Beaufort; isolation is contrasted with community, and exposure with security.

The articulation between *Georgetown* and the next image, *Bar – Las Vegas, Nevada,* is again wonderfully complex. There is certainly a *caesura.* Extending further the musical analogies discussed above, the notion of this musical pause, a momentary cessation, a break in the flow for reflection, consideration and to collect oneself ahead of the following activity, is a useful comparison. *Bar, Nevada* includes no children or older people. This is the first time in many images that these have not been represented. Its lone character is a mature male. Moreover, the photograph initiates a sequence of images that signally juxtapose poverty and affluence. It is clearly a break, then, but Frank continues to weave his work together. Across this thematic break, he creates a pictorial triptych. The central image of the three is *Georgetown,* the two women and the child, as we have already noted, forming a triangular composition that can be related to Renaissance religious paintings. This, you will recall, was preceded by a photograph of a lone black child, to the right of the centre of the image with a jukebox off to the left. The third image echoes this; *Bar, Nevada* having an Hispanic man occupying the central ground with a jukebox off to the right. In its provision of a few minutes of enculturating wisdom, each song being a message from the elevated world of pop stars and folk singers for the price of a nickel or a dime, the jukebox has an almost religious profundity and influence. It replaces, perhaps, the angelic messengers of God. It is appropriate, then, that these mechanical seraphs should feature as bracketing photographs for a composition characteristic of depictions of the holy family.

Bar, Nevada depicts an impoverished space. The room is empty of people and mostly empty of furniture. Its floor, of linoleum perhaps, is tattered around the edges. The walls are empty of images of any kind, no advertisements or pictures. The lone man in the centre, dressed in a patterned shirt and dark trousers, provides, along with the jukebox, the only life apparent in the place. His body language is lackadaisical and uncertain.

He is followed by an image of a solid and affluent couple in a *Hotel Lobby – Miami Beach*. The woman is wrapped in mink and sports large earrings. Her pose communicates casual confidence, while her companion is quietly threatening in his dour self-belief. The overall impression is of assuredness and comfort, in stark contrast to the uncertainty and visual poverty of the previous photograph.

After figuring affluence and poverty as evidenced by people, Frank presents us with a pair of pictures that demonstrate affluence and poverty in the landscape. *View from hotel window – Butte, Montana* images sooty roofs receding between gray, rain-slicked roads, the whole outlook framed by grubby hotel voiles. This work holds, in silver nitrate, the sooty heart of industrial America. The photograph also refers to and plays with some of the promotional images used by Standard Oil, in its widely disseminated publicity campaigns. This is, interestingly, the first image in *The Americans* without any people.

We turn the page to another landscape, this time recording the *Metropolitan Life Insurance Building – New York City.* Instead of grimy curtains and streets on an overcast day, we see a multitude of windows set into the curves of a dove-grey building, many of them reflecting the brilliance of this very different day. In the foreground are a streetlight and a news-stand, the latter featuring a copy of *Bazaar*, the magazine that was formerly Frank's employer. Other titles are there too: *See, Paris Life, Art, Man's, Western, Seventeen* and *Companion*. The serried ranks of magazines visually echo the rising tiers of windows in the building behind. This is a tongue-in-cheek autobiographical photograph, its message contained in its title; this is the metropolitan life of New York, which was for so many years Frank's home. We noted earlier Frank's acknowledged dislike and eventual rejection of his work as a magazine photographer. He disliked the idea of 'hack' photojournalism, intent on the pursuit of notoriety and the security of money:

> I also wanted to follow my own intuition and do it my way, and not make concessions—not make a *Life* story. That was another thing I hated. (Frank, in Janis and MacNeil 1977: 56)

His implication in this photograph's amusing juxtaposition of ranks of magazines with ranks of windows in the four square building is obvious: work for a magazine if you want the security of metropolitan success and acknowledgement.

Moving on now from the juxtaposition of poverty and affluence that had occupied him through the last several images, Frank chooses to reinforce his critique of magazines in case we might have missed the point. The next image features another magazine, this time emblazoned 'Awake!' It is in the hands of a *Jehovah's Witness – Los Angeles*, who is standing alone in front of the dove-gray stones of just such a building as was depicted in the last photograph. Away from the massed throng of photojournalistic output, of whatever shade, that filled the previous image's news-stand, we see this less commercial, cheaper publication, carrying this uncertain older man's faith. The image ascribes little nobility to the Witness, its tilted perspective rendering him somewhat foreshortened. He seems apologetic, even threatened, perhaps. Nonetheless, his cheap and tawdry looking publication is an aspect of his sincerity, and is unlikely to ever make his fortune.

The links through the next three images are restrained. *Jehovah's Witness* has a horizon line that slides down from left to right. The following image, *Bar – New Mexico*, pictures a blurred interior in which the dominant line travels up from left to right, balancing the earlier image. *Bar*, like *Jehovah's Witness*, also depicts a central male figure, standing in the middle ground. *Bar*, though, has two other men flanking the central figure, their bodies filling the photograph's foreground with dark silhouettes. The cowboy-hatted man lacks the uncertainty of the *Jehovah's Witness* and is at his ease. The camera's low position, below waist height, suggests that the image may have been captured surreptitiously, and further reinforces the possibility of tension.

I see no discernible direct connection through the next two images. This is evidence, perhaps, of Frank's stated hatred of stories with clearly discernible narratives. The wealth of connections elsewhere, though, must leave this lack open to question—hopefully someone else will solve this riddle.

U.S. 30 between Ogallala and North Platte, Nebraska depicts four houses, a telegraph pole and a letterbox on a prairie, seen from the road. As we have seen, many contemporary travellers from Europe saw exactly these unremarkable highway moments as the defining images of America. *U.S. 30* and the following image of a female gambler beneath a burned-out light in *Casino – Elko, Nevada* defeat all but my most basic attempts at sequential connection. A victory, perhaps, for Frank?

With some relief then, given this section's intent, the next photograph, *U.S. 91, leaving Blackfoot, Idaho*, begins a sequence of five images concerned with the iconography of the car. These introduce an extended consideration of new and representative icons of American civilization, which lasts for the next fifteen images.

The car is a major strophe within *The Americans*, representing, along with a number of other objects, the explosion of affordable consumer goods, growing out of the innovations of the 'American System of Manufactures'. This system of standardized and mechanized production was instituted by manufacturers in the nineteenth century, and was principally a result of the requirements of US Government acquisitions (Mayr and Post 1981). Initially focused on military items, the advantages of uniformity are obvious, both in terms of user familiarity and the possibility of field repair of damaged equipment. This latter was vital in a country as large and as thinly populated as the United States. The government's insistence on the 'interchangeability of parts' was also significantly supported by sizeable grants of public money for research and development. Places like Smith's Armoury in Connecticut pioneered the approach, and it was quickly adopted by manufacturers of guns, sewing machines and then automobiles. 'Mass production' was seen to require the liberal use of machines in order to achieve the desired tolerances, and resulted in identical objects of good quality. These lacked the distinction of smaller-scale, hand-finished manufacture. Making functional goods available to everyone at a fraction of the cost of their hand-made, luxurious equivalents had enormous consequences for society. Not the least of these was the slow acquisition by America of the leadership of the industrialized world. Europe clung too long to the notion of 'class distinction through consumption', in which items were clearly and deliberately manufactured for particular social segments. The inertia of European manufacturing caused by its long traditions and craft basis also contributed, and greatly damaged Europe's competitiveness, leaving the field clear for the United States. American society is mostly financially stratified, and the notion of restricting access to goods on the basis of birth was not functional there. The flux created by mass immigration was too unstable for concerns regarding 'appropriate consumption' to triumph. This made America a prime market for mass-produced goods. Frank examines these consumables and industrial artefacts in the next fifteen images, beginning here with the car and the road.

America did not have a monopoly on the automobile. It was developed in Europe by pioneers like Mercedes and Rolls Royce, but these vehicles were expensive luxury items available only to the socially elite. Hitler's Volkswagen, the 'people's car' was an attempt to democratize car ownership, but these were not widely available in the post-war Europe which Frank experienced. Nonetheless, European photographers did create images analogous to those made by Frank in America. I especially like those of Margaret Tudor-Hart. The enormous difference in America was the affordability of the car and its consequent pervasion into far more of society than was at that time evident elsewhere.

U.S. 91, leaving Blackfoot, Idaho shows two intense young men, one of them driving Frank's car. They speed forward, focused on the road and on their destination. The middle passenger, between Frank and the driver, is almost claustrophobically close to the camera. These headlong, hell-for-leather men are followed by *St. Petersburg, Florida.* Although this image was taken far from Idaho, Frank's sequencing gives us the impression that these same drivers could be at the wheel of the speed-blurred sedan in the upper part of the image. In the foreground, a group of old people waits, stationary, seated on benches, on the sidewalk, safely away from the speeding car. The contrast between the imperative energy of youth and the calm stasis of age is marked, and is a part of Frank's consideration of the car as a conduit of human experience.

If we have any remaining doubts about the religious allusions in Frank's work, then *Covered car – Long Beach, California* lays them to rest. The caption seems a little redundant, given the clarity with which the car is imaged. It serves, though, to remove any uncertainty as to the photograph's subject. The framing palm trees are portico like, and supply a temple precinct for the automobile 'altar', complete with its altar cloth. Is this too fanciful? Is it too much to read all of this into a photograph of a car on a street in California? The image that follows, *Car accident – U.S. 66, between Winslow and Flagstaff Arizona*, removes any doubt. Here, beneath a blanket or tarpaulin, on a cold day in the semi-desert, lie the victims of a car crash. It is a dour and sombre image, revealing for us the victims sacrificed on the altar of the car. This is the price paid for mass transit and the much-beloved American desire for the freedom to chase the Dream. These two images echo each other compositionally as well, with the long, low shape of the covered car echoed by the covered bodies. The image Frank chose for inclusion is sombre, respectful and reverential: Frank's contact sheet reveals the full random horror and misery of the fatal collision.

The freedom of the road is powerfully evidenced in the next image, *U.S. 285, New Mexico*. This image reveals a shining road, reflecting light off its tyre-polished surface, running arrow-straight through the dark and featureless New Mexico landscape, beneath a dark and lowering sky. The road runs straight up to the horizon, appearing to rise vertically in the extreme distance and to prick the sky, cascading images of heavenly glory behind the dark veil, evoking the opening of a fairy gate for America's enchanted children. One instantly suspects some darkroom interference here, given New Mexico's climate and the light bouncing off the blacktop. Some writers, Kerouac included (in Frank 1959: 2), see this as a moonlit shot, but I do not find the argument convincing due to the intensity of the road-reflected light. The camera, also, is positioned in the road, and a long exposure, though certainly possible on this little-used stretch of road, would be problematic. Frank's contact sheet confirms that this was a daylight shot.

Clearly the car and the road are powerful icons of American civilization, and they lead easily into the following ten depictions of other icons of American culture. John Szarkowski, with characteristic insight, describes Frank's depiction of these in his recollections on the rear cover of the 1968 Aperture edition of *The Americans*:

> Frank established a new iconography for contemporary America, comprised of bits of bus depots, lunch counters, strip developments, empty spaces, cars, and unknowable facts. (Szarkowski, in Frank 1968: rear cover)

From the wilderness of New Mexico, we plunge straight into *Bar – Detroit*, which introduces the third chapter. This is pure *On the Road*, which so frequently juxtaposes the boggling immensity of the American hinterland with just such intimate and human spaces. The photograph records the upper part of one of the bar's walls and its ceiling. Mounted above some faux half-timbering is a relief model of the American flag blowing in the wind, centrally mounted between portraits of Washington and Lincoln. The serious and solemn dead presidents overlook the world whose creation they contributed to. There is no sense of irony in their placing; the bar (which we cannot see) is part of the America they represent. Their *gravitas* heightens the contrast between the framed, traditional portraits and the flag that sits between them. It is captured in mid-flap, frozen in what appears to be vacuum-moulded plastic. It is illuminated, its warm reassuring heart spotlighted, or powered perhaps by a bulb burning within. The works of the painters' hands and the work of the plastic moulding machine sit together on the wall, both accepted as contributors and representatives of national identity. There are other signs sitting beneath this triptych. 'You must be 21 and prove' says one, revealing this as an adult world. Next to it hangs a faux hunting trophy, featuring a cartoon-like smiling fish. The kitsch, the cheap and the tacky sit comfortably next to the nation's dearest symbols. They are thus elevated into the orbit of presidents and become, by association and because of Frank's vision, similarly invested with identity. Equally, the presidents and the flag are levelled by proximity to the ephemeral and the insignificant.

Barber shop through screen door – McClellanville, South Carolina is another clear depiction of a celebrated American icon. Frank is referencing his mentor Walker Evans' work here, whose *Barbershop, Havana* (1933, estate of Walker Evans) similarly depicted just such an interior. This image is unremarkable in many ways, typically Frank in its referencing, typically Frank in its identification and presentation of an American symbol and typically Frank in the photograph's contribution to the wider structuring and intentionality of *The Americans*. There is, though, something that sets this image apart. In some ways it is Frank's pictorial signature, his thesis statement for the book. He communicates this by the manner in which we are shown the interior of the barber shop. We don't just see through the window, we see into the shop through the shadow cast by Frank's head and shoulders as he holds his camera. This falls on to a screen door which is reflecting the street scene opposite, a number of unremarkable houses and hedges across a road. We only see the barber's chair and ranged bottles because of Frank's shadow. He is showing us that this is the America he sees, a shifting and mercurial place only captured according to his vision, and, literally in this case, seen through his head and his Leica. Not just here but throughout *The Americans*, we are seeing the world that Frank saw, the roads he walked, the cars he drove, the people and the things that filled his days. He is contained by, but here also containing, America. Despite its significance, this photograph fits perfectly into the sequence: the barber shop is an American symbol, an icon, and it continues the study.

Backyard – Venice West, California is another complex image. It combines a suggestion of the Stars and Stripes in the striped tarpaulin that is sheltering an old man in his garden with an image of a derelict and redundant car. This is an automotive analogy for the final days that the old man is clearly experiencing. The flag-like tarpaulin over the man recalls Cartier-Bresson's *New England* (1933, collection of Magnum). For the geriatrics in both of these photographs, life, with all its struggles and joys, has not left them at all resistant to their national symbol.

Newburgh, New York pictures a biker on his motorcycle. There appears to be an expression of hostility and suspicion in its subject's face, an expression much beloved by Frank. Two similarly garbed associates flank the rider, suggesting perhaps a biker's club. One of these wears a badged hat, reminiscent of the one worn by Marlon Brando as he played the leader of just such a biker gang in *The Wild One* (Benedek 1954). The film carried messages of freedom from convention and examined personal revolution in a trammelled and conformist society. These were expressions of the same motivations that fuelled the Beats, notwithstanding the clear visual and philosophically differences. The look is archetypal '50s chic, and the motorcyclist bears a striking, and amusing, resemblance to the singer George Michael, who would later adopt this same image for a while. His aping of this style reflects the contemporary importation into Europe of American motorcycle culture, mixing Harley Davidsons and Hell's Angels with, in England, the indigenous 'ton-up' boys with their Vincents, Nortons and Enfields. My father was such a biker.

Continuing his examination of essential American icons, Frank next presents *Luncheonette – Butte, Montana.* This relatively minimal photograph pictures at centre a gaming table. It looks similar to a pool table, save that it has only two pockets, each flanked by mushroom-shaped wooden pieces, with a further eight such pieces in the table's centre, forming the shape of a cross. Typically in Frank's structuring of *The Americans*, this cross-image anticipates a new visual strophe, which will take over from these icons in seven images' time. For now, though, it is enough that the cross is a part of this table, the kind of diner furniture featured so liberally in *The Wild One* and *Rebel Without a Cause* (Ray 1955), arguably the first significant 'teen movie'. Behind the table is a series of equally powerful American objects: campaign bills advertising candidates for state and county office. This level of democracy, the election of particular administrative officials, was and still is uncommon in Europe. In England, for example, the electorate does not vote directly for the prime minister, for financial officers (like the state treasurer pasted to this wall), or for members of the legislature, like the attorneys, both general and county, pictured in this photograph. Democracy is always faux, but in England it is a semblance, a simulacrum and a sham. Democracy is also, of course, one of the mostly widely traded and most seriously compromised ideas with which America seeks to be associated.

The wooden 'mushrooms' on the table, and the oblique angle of the tabletop, are visually echoed in the next image, *Santa Fe, New Mexico.* Here, petrol pumps stand like one-armed automata beneath a giant sign saying 'Save'. The clearly financial intention of the gas station's creators' sign is altered by Frank's image into an allusion to salvation. It is a practical salvation offered by this essential watering hole in the hugely extensive desert, but it carries other implications. The Christian notion of salvation is clearly invoked, giving to this collection of tin and paint the significance of an ecclesiastical construction. The shamrocks on the petrol pumps' 'heads', a symbol of luck from old Irish folklore, extend this notion further, and the arrangement of pumps fancifully echoes the stone circles of Neolithic peoples. These are new circles, in a new world, created for itself by a new civilization.

Bar – New York City is the notably vague caption for the next image. The icon featured here has been seen several times already: it is the jukebox. In this photograph, though, Frank's communication of his understanding of this object is as clear as it ever gets. The robot-like jukebox sits in an unremarkable bar, in front of a partition, across from customers sitting at a table. A further customer is just caught, motion blurred, as he leaves the frame. The jukebox at the heart of this photograph glows, its inner light reminiscent of the engines of spaceships in contemporary science fiction films, or images of nuclear fission carried by myriad popular magazines. It lights up the place like an angelic visitor, a modern-day Gabriel trumpeting in song the arrival of a new age, to an almost entirely indifferent audience.

Elevator – Miami Beach is a rather more difficult image to place in this sequence. It questions, as always with Frank's work, whether or not the understanding I'm peddling is mistaken, and invites you to restrain your credulity. The photograph is certainly full of clear aspects of America. The woman blurred to the left wears a fur stole, and her affluence and freedom contrast markedly with the bondage-through-need of the elevator operator. This contrast between rich and poor is one of Frank's concerns throughout the work. Elevators were certainly not restricted to America, and whether this image truly includes anything that is 'iconic' is questionable. Is this another *caesura*, another moment that checks the flow, lest it descend into some loathsome, programmatic Aristotelian unity? Perhaps. It is certainly a powerful image, and fits easily into this extended consideration of the *stigmata* of America.

Religion is becoming ever more pronounced in these images of American icons. The following photograph, *Restaurant – U.S. 1 leaving Columbia, South Carolina*, pictures a diner, one of the iconic forms repeatedly photographed by Frank. The clean table reflects an intense light, streaming in from the window. The room is entirely empty of people. There is, though, a shirt, tie and jacketed man on the TV. He is not identified here, but Frank's re-use of this image elsewhere, as we have discussed already, identified him as the evangelist Oral Roberts. As a TV preacher, he is presumably preaching about something that he might call 'light', on a tube illuminated by the bombardment of florescent spots by billions of streaming electrons, all this in a room filled with brilliant sunlight. Again, the simulacrum is contrasted with the reality. Significantly, on this glorious day, there is no one to hear Roberts preach. They are all outside –all of them, that is, except the man behind the camera.

As well as continuing the 'icons' theme and further examining the religious nature of these icons, *Drive-in movie – Detroit* also features light as a major aspect. The next three images are linked by lighting, all of them being taken in the 'golden hour' of sunrise/sunset. *Drive-in movie* captures flickering characters on a large screen, watched by a couple in a cabriolet and innumerable others whose presence we must assume, hidden as they are inside their sedans. The film's plaid-shirted protagonist, occupying perhaps a twelfth of the image, is intent on something in his screen-bounded reality. He seems insignificant and faintly ridiculous against the vastness of the evening sky. Frank's photograph reveals the little human world in its insularity and self-obsession, ephemeral and insignificant against the enormity of this, and every, evening.

The crowd's serried attention in the drive-in is contrasted sharply with a lone man in the next photograph, who is looking away into the sunset. He is wearing white robes, which distance him from the workaday and contemporary, clearly in a deliberate act of demarcation. His simple white cross, and the book from which he reads, denote a Christian element to his devotions. He appears to be praying, as the *Mississippi River, Baton Rouge, Louisiana* flows ponderously by, mirroring the light from the evening sky. The man we see praying was known for his practice of walking up and down the river as a pilgrimage, praying as he went. Frank encountered him at a ferry crossing, moving around the cars as they waited for and then boarded the boat. Frank has pictured him away from even that restrained action, thereby heightening the sense of solitude. This is one of the few photographs of traditional religious observance or imagery in *The Americans* that does not raise an eyebrow or wag a finger in consternation. I wonder, though, how aware the pilgrim was of himself as Frank's subject: a photographer and he together on the riverbank. Was he complicit in the creation of the picture? Although Frank has shown repeatedly that he embraces, and offers no apology for, his presence and his shaping vision, there would be irony in one of *The Americans*' most sincere photographs being essentially staged.

St Francis, gas station and City Hall – Los Angeles also bathe in a quiet sun. This hazy light is, I suspect, in the early morning, given the geography of the image. The hulking building at left is not City Hall, as the statue is not of St Francis, but the rise in ground level to the right suggests that the image is looking from west to east, across what was then Sunset Boulevard (this section of road was later renamed Victor Chavez Highway in honour of the public figure). The duplicity within the image raises questions certainly, but it does not destroy the power of the depiction. This robed man (St Junipero Serra, in fact), cross held high, church clutched under his arm, is preaching passionately to the rising sun, to a highway and to a car lot. Temporal power, represented by City Hall (had it been City Hall), has moved away from the gospel of this preacher, cut off by the road, separated by the technology of travel. St Francis famously preached to the captivated birds. In this image, even the cars look somnolent, distant and disinterested. The tiny church beneath his arm also seems anachronistic in this world of pistons, rubber and asphalt.

Light again streams down on to *Crosses at scene of highway accident – U.S. 91, Idaho*. The light is unnatural looking, most probably the result of a fault or crack in the lens (see the discussion of Frank's possible use of a cracked lens in '*The tools*' in Chapter 2). The intense centre beam, flanked by two fainter subsidiaries, recalls many

Renaissance depictions of the opening of heaven and the descent of the Holy Spirit. Titian's *Assumption of the Virgin* (1516–18, Basilica di Santa Maria Gloriosa dei Frari, Venice) is an example. For me, though, the most poignant resonance is with Rembrandt's powerful etching *Three Crosses*. In both Frank's and Rembrandt's work, this light-from-above falls on to three crosses. The ones in Frank's photograph are small, possibly metal, cruciforms, stuck into the verge of the highway mentioned. Most likely, it is a roadside memorial for people fallen in just such a road accident as was figured earlier between *Winslow and Flagstaff, Arizona*. Here, in a place which a moment's inattention would miss, Frank has discovered the contemporary world's refiguring of the image underlying the iconography of the crucifixion. Rembrandt's suffering Christ and broken beggars are gone now, and these tin memorials are left, along with those they remember, silent and alone in the vastness of the American heartland.

Almost unavoidably, the next image echoes its predecessor in the placement at the top centre of another block of light. This time it is artificial, falling from overhead incandescents, illuminating a factory production line. Frank, as usual, is not content with this single linking motif. Given the interdependence of human beings in a society such as the one he was examining, these two images also discuss something of the range and variety of social relationships in the country at this time. *Assembly line – Detroit* is not overtly a car factory, but the implication is powerful, given the position of the photograph in Frank's book and Detroit's notable pre-eminence in the American car industry. Black and white workers are busy alongside each other in their artificial world, labouring to construct the vehicles that ultimately claim the lives of people like those remembered overleaf. The car, rather than the cross, is the wheel on which they are broken.

The social articulation explored in *Crosses* and *Detroit* instigates a short section of images that explore 'the faces of the leaders and the faces of followers' as Frank described it in his funding application (Frank, in Greenough 2009: 362).

The overalled workers of *Detroit*'s heavy industry are followed by a picture of a crowd of smartly dressed men in *Convention hall – Chicago*. Their earnest activity, name tags and indecipherable button badges give the event the look of a political convention, but this is not anywhere stated. What is clear is that the huddle of men in the right foreground is engaged in apparently sensitive negotiations. The central figure, who has his back to the camera, is surrounded by three others. Of the two we can see, one is looking downwards with concern and the other, cigar in hand, is conciliatory and placating, while retaining an air of invulnerable confidence. Behind these figures, another older man is pointing in a confrontational and accusatory manner. Behind this foreground huddle is a hall brimful with faces, all front-facing. These are mostly, though not exclusively, male. We can't know the details of the American policy, perhaps, or personnel movement, or financial shenanigans at the heart of this moment, but the universality of the political instinct in human beings is presented for us here, with all its partiality, dissemblance and compromise. The contrast with the previous page is marked. These clean-shaven, suited and self-satisfied men are the balance to the busy labourers of the previous image. Each is tied to the other, with bindings invisible to the eye, certainly, but as certain as steel. Even though they are never likely to meet, they are symbiotic, mutely dependent. In the American capitalist industrial system, the financiers and powerbrokers rely on the labourers, just as the labourers, more or less willingly, sought their lesser gains in the enterprises of the entrepreneurs. Perhaps symbiosis is too good a word, since each cooperating organism should benefit equally from the relationship. This is clearly not so here. We cannot call the convention attendees parasitic, either, since the factory in Detroit could not have run without them.

Men's room, railway station – Memphis, Tennessee swoops down from the acquisitive and moneyed world of the last image into what Kerouac called 'the loneliest picture ever made, the urinals that women never see, the shoeshine going on in sad eternity' (Kerouac, in Frank 1959: 5). A blue-collar worker certainly, stooping and overalled, is cleaning the shoes of a suited man enthroned on a high seat. The chair was clearly constructed to save the back of the cleaner, but emphasizes thereby the difference in their stations. The suited man hides his face with his hand as if he, like Kerouac, is aware that this is a scene not meant for universal consumption, a secret place of sorts. Perhaps he is aware, too, of the lowliness of the moment. The cleaner's implements lie around the men's room, reminding us of his other duties: he tends the feet and the urinals of others. The loneliness of which Kerouac speaks is palpable, but it is not all that is here. The toilets are clean and well maintained and the attendant seems engaged in his work. We tend to pity those we feel are less fortunate than ourselves and, if we are sympathetic, to look down from our self-assumed positions of superiority and castigate ourselves for our complicity in their situations and circumstances. Kerouac stops short of this but the scent of it is in his commentary. This is not necessarily true in Frank's image, however: no one asked the attendant how he felt.

The subterranean, hidden world of the men's room leads into a *Cocktail party – New York City*. The people pictured are not overtly workers, although social networking is, of course, an essential aspect of business. The men at extreme left and right are smart and taut, framing the women in the centre of the photograph. They are smiling and polite, their body language suggesting mannered and superficial engagement with each other, with only the woman second from left implying any kind of real intimacy. These wealthy and leisured individuals present yet another face of the complex social interrelationships that characterize, and weave between, the Americans Frank is observing.

Salt Lake City, Utah is another of those wonderfully anomalous images that serve to disrupt Frank's work and dam the sequential flow of his images. It is a real maverick, having little relationship to any of the other photographs in the work. It is an architectural photograph, so relates vaguely to other photographs dominated by buildings, such as *Rooming House – Bunker Hill, Los Angeles*. *Salt Lake City* pictures a darkly sinister building. We can easily see from its signboard that it is an Art School, however much it may resemble the Bates Motel from Alfred Hitchcock's celebrated film *Psycho* (1960). The low light renders the entrance gate, the steps and the roofline an almost-silhouette against the pale sky. Amusingly, the image is a study in shapes, the rectangular noticeboard, spherical gate ornament and the conical roof of the tower all describing the geometry that Cezanne believed was at the heart of all of nature and that, through him, powerfully influenced the development of Euro-American art in the twentieth century. Is that all this is, a quick smile between Frank's other considerations? A momentary nod, perhaps, in his inimitable way to Moholy-Nagy and others, for whom geometry and form were of the most pressing significance? A formalist moment discovered by Frank in the nether lands of America? However we understand it, it is a moment in his progression around the country, and is an intriguing and unsettling pause in our progress through the book.

Beaufort, South Carolina, is another tricky image. There is little direct relationship between it and its predecessor, revealing a black woman sitting outside in another sunset. She, her chair and a high distant cross are the only marks of humanity on this landscape. She is looking off to the right, smiling. The cross, as we noted, was a major linking element in several earlier photographs and is reprised here. It prefigures the next image in a way, since the following photograph is the first of three images of death. The cross strophe/theme also surfaces in another image nine on from this one, where it is even more overtly linked with death. That image too is stranded, offering no immediate, direct connections with its neighbours. The palpable peace of the sitting woman smiling into the evening, at rest in her chair, contrasts powerfully with the following images of life's extinction. How rare are these moments of satisfied stasis, in the dynamic, uncertain and never-resting experience we all share, heading headlong, if so often indiscernibly, for the grave? How is it possible in the flood, carried as we are on the tide of our experience, to rest and be at peace? In this image, Frank records someone who has found a moment of it. Kerouac described her as, 'One incredible I think Seminole woman pulling on her cigarette with thoughts of her own, as pure a picture as the nicest tenor solo in jazz' (Kerouac in Frank 1959: 3).

All that notwithstanding, she is cheek by jowl with *Funeral – St. Helena, South Carolina.* Frank has images of death before in his book: this is the second one taken at this event and bearing this title. In the first *St. Helena* image, the faces of the mourners reflect death as they lean on their cars. It is found, also, lying beneath a tarpaulin on the *U.S. 66 between Winslow and Flagstaff.* In this second *St. Helena*, the faces of the black men we can see are looking down, two of them at the floor, one of them contemplating the corpse. The manicured dead man is smartly dressed and appears as though he is sleeping. The expression of the man in the foreground mixes curiosity and empathy with fear. This contemplation creates a connection between the young man, standing tall along the left hand side of the image, and the dead man lying to the right. Together they constitute the foreground plane of the picture, from which the other mourners stand back. The obvious tension between a young, living black man and an older one, now dead, examines and contrasts life and death. Their similar suits, the light fitting overhead and the burned out materiality of the photograph itself all serve to locate this profound moment of passing in a room in St Helena, South Carolina, in the mid '50s. The mourners celebrate all that this man has been and all that he has meant to the world. Frank communicates the profundity of this moment, amongst all of this ephemera, through his use of light. A good part of the image is burned out. The sky outside the building in which the dead man is lying is brilliant, this same light eating into the adjacent vegetation and haloing the men on the sunward side of the group. The floor of the building is similarly brilliant, biting at the edges of the coffin and the trousers of the men next to it. This invocation of light and darkness occurs very often in the rites of passage from life to death. From the burning of burial ships by Northern Europeans to the Ghats of the Ganges, humanity associates light with life and celebrates that light in the rituals of life's ending. This isn't surprising: the creation and control of light are limited to very few species of animals and the manipulation of fire to only one, light and fire thus being appropriate sigils for our species. Invoking them for a human passing is entirely appropriate. The echoes in this photograph of other, older memorials are no mistake.

Frank's image is interestingly foreshadowed by the wonderful portrait of *Victor Hugo on his deathbed* by Nadar (F. Nadar, 1885, J. Paul Getty Museum). The celebrated nineteenth century French portraitist uses light, streaming from above, to stunning effect, communicating an engagement with the 'transcendent unknown' that we all contemplate, at some point or other and most often in the presence or environs of death. Frank figures this mystical signifier in *St. Helena,* just as he figured it earlier, shining down on *Crosses at scene of highway accident – U.S. 91, Idaho.*

The busy funeral contrasts markedly with the next image, *Chinese cemetery – San Francisco.* During one of the city's famous fogs, Frank has photographed a jumble of wreaths and white-painted sticks: one assumes that this was a standing tribute of some sort, now collapsed. Indistinct in the foreground are white shapes, which look like Chinese character-bearing prayer papers, but might equally be fallen flowers or leaves. A line of windswept conifers tapers away across the sky of the upper part of the image. The broken earth of the burial is contained within a wooden former of some sort, describing an 'L' shape on the ground within the photograph. These hard geometrical shapes are the marks of man, drawn beneath the enormity of this ocean-born, foggy sky. In this palpably damp and lonely space, they are ineffectual, peremptory and perfunctory. This is the end of all life, dust to dust, ashes to ashes, and the end, also, of all memorials. As Thomas Hardy so wonderfully expressed it in his *During Wind and Rain,* 'Down their carved names the raindrop plows' (Hardy 1917). Kerouac, in his introduction, also senses the loneliness: 'blown over Chinese cemetery flowers in a San Francisco hill being hammered by potatopatch fog on a March night I'd say nobody there but the rubber cat' (Kerouac, in Frank 1959: 6).

So, then, to the book's final 'section', initiated again by an image of a flag. We have noted that the previous three sections featured many thematically linked sequences of images. There are some such sequences in this section also, but the dominant structural device here is the use of linkages between adjacent images, usually one referring back to the previous image and another referring to the subsequent image. In some cases, these links are strong enough to constitute a themed pair, but in many instances they are simply visual echoes.

After the melancholy of the Chinese cemetery, *Political rally – Chicago* is a witty photograph, with an almost jokey sense to it. It reveals a Sousaphone player, his head obscured by his instrument, playing beneath a flag. Sousa, child of a nineteenth century European family, is equally famous for his marching band music and for adding the letters USA to his real name 'So'. The depersonalization of this musician by his decapitation leaves him, too, absorbed into America, his body supporting an enormous horn beneath the flag. He is the perfect mouthpiece for the rally, which, we can only assume, is happening around this horn's *recitative*. There are echoes of Cartier-Bresson here in the wry humour of the depiction. Frank's import, though, is entirely other. Contact sheets (Greenough 2009: 376–77) show that this image is from the same event as the earlier *Political Rally – Chicago* photograph, that one featuring a gesticulating man apparently in an ecstasy of declamation. In this later image of the rally, all we see is a man who has given himself entirely to his role, losing even his face and with it his individuality. Further, this photograph significantly echoes *Parade – Hoboken,* which started Frank's book. There, the flag obscures the face of a reserved and nervous woman, her hand held to her mouth in suppression, perhaps, of the misgivings she feels, as a parade celebrating her world passes by. Both of these Americans are lost to the flag, both partially absorbed into its colours. The difference is their complicity: the first seems ambivalent and uncertain; the latter is fully committed to his immolation.

Store window – Washington, D.C. continues the political theme, although subtly. A mannequin sporting a formal suit provides the link: it, too, is headless. The dummy advertises the shop's business; its 'Formal Wear' sign is visible at the top of the image. For some reason, the shop front's window is missing, replaced by what appears to be plastic sheeting. A refit is, perhaps, being undertaken. This creates an intriguing and beguiling uncertainty in the image's depiction of depth. After consideration, it becomes clear that the political portrait, which looks like Dwight Eisenhower, is stuck to this plastic, causing it to curtain. This disembodied head, which floats in the confusing space adjacent to the headless mannequin, is a bizarre echo of a gallery-hung painting, or a display box filled with curiosities. Robert Rauschenberg's constructions, such as *Coca-Cola Plan* (R. Rauschenburg, 1958, Museum of Contemporary Art, Los Angeles) made political, social and aesthetic points through the collection and juxtaposition of found objects. These would come two years after these photographs. Frank finds something similar in this apparently innocent, 'found' moment.

As the headless bandsman leads us to the headless mannequin, so the pasted photograph of a disembodied head on the shop front vignette leads us into *Television studio – Burbank, California*. Here, a very real presenter at left looks across Frank's image at a monitor showing her disembodied head, vignetted by the TV screen. Frank is playing with levels of reality and artifice in this picture. Neither of the presenters is real, obviously, one is recorded directly onto 35mm silver halide film while the other arrived via cathode ray tubes and radio waves. The image includes another visual joke. The television studio set uses a series of linked diamond shapes suspended at either side of the presenter, to frame her space. The angle Frank has chosen for his photograph renders these diamonds arrow-like. Her gaze seems to follow these arrows from her studio seat to the screen on which she appears, as if she is watching and musing on her projected self. The arrows also serve to illustrate, in a way redolent of '50s graphics, the process by which she is captured by the camera and 'delivered' to the TV set.

Los Angeles catches the arrow fired from *Burbank*, on the side of an otherwise dismal, featureless building. This is one of my favourite images in *The Americans*, speaking so concisely and so eloquently of our species' hunger for meaning and direction, within a mass of indifferent dark shapes and dead ends. The neon arrow glows in the shadows of the claustrophobic street, pointing, apparently, at nothing, leading perhaps nowhere, but demonstrating such certainty and confidence, such brilliant poise and self-belief as it burns amidst the dirty and beaten bricks and stones. It is a theme we've seen before in *Jay – New York* and in the fatuous faces of politicians in *Hoboken*. A torn, tattered and compromised reality is whitewashed over and adorned with bright distractions. This is the heart of the America Frank has come to know. As he wrote:

> I was aware that I was living in a different world—that the world wasn't as good as that—that it was a myth that the sky was blue and that all photographs were beautiful. (Frank, in Johnson 1989: 37)

There is no blue sky in *Los Angeles*, and the nature and quality of the American myth is revealed and celebrated wonderfully in this image. I can't help but think on the iconic quality of the mark-making in Jackson Pollock, Willem de Kooning or Alfred Leslie's painting, each of them seeking to identify and exploit just such significant symbols. The arrow is a profound and recurring symbol in human culture. I generally avoid the notion of the 'universal', limited as our intelligence necessarily is to the viewpoint of men, but if we accept that limitation, this somewhat spurious notion may be invoked here. The arrow takes us back to the days of stone and has been inscribed by us for millennia on walls of rock, wherever we have passed. Frank's photograph continues and comments on that tradition. It lacks the dignity of time that petroglyphs claim, and doesn't even have the elevated context of a gallery-displayed painting. This, of course, is its strength. Frank has caught this unself-consciously human moment, in which a sign is at once openly deceitful in its masking of the sooty reality beneath and almost noble in its relationship to the walking man following its direction. Let's think again of Camus' model of nobility, described through Sisyphus, who is doomed to roll his stone always up the hill, only to see it fall each evening back to the starting point. Sisyphus, nonetheless, smiles his defiance into the teeth of the indifferent Fates and rolls once more. This solitary man on a sidewalk in Los Angeles is, in his own striding way, engaged in exactly as noble a pursuit. As a footnote, it's worth remembering that Los Angeles is naturally a place of blue skies. This image must be either a twilight shot, which is consistent with the glowing neon, or might be taken beneath the city's smog, or during the famous 'June gloom'.

The tenuous connections within this section continue, with only the notion of the solitary man linking the previous image with *Bank – Houston, Texas.* Here, a suited, bald man sits behind a solid desk, at the rear of a room full of vacant, opulently upholstered chairs arranged around other solid desks. On one of the desks in the middle distance sits, incongruously, a hat. The direction and appearance of determination and dynamism in the previous image are juxtaposed with clutter and stasis here. A grimy backstreet, which might be the setting for a certain kind of heroism, is contrasted here with the trappings of opulence, and a man contained, motionless, like a caged pet, in his moneyed world.

We've noted that Frank wished to contrast white-collar and blue-collar workers, and he continues to do that with the next photograph, following a man who appears to be a bank clerk with an image of an overalled man in *Factory – Detroit.* The photograph is mostly filled with a wall, stretching away towards a gas-containing tower in the distance. Frank is standing in what appears to be an entrance, with a workbench, complete with engineer's vice, almost obscured in the shadows. Three steel bollards, sunk into the concrete pavement, protect the wall and are scored with marks left by passing vehicles. The lone man is sitting against the wall, looking quizzically, perhaps suspiciously, at Frank. He wears a hat, again linking this image into the last one. This time it is an engineer's cap, favoured by such iconic TV characters as Casey Jones, the heroic railway man, solving problems and saving America from chaos in every town through which his engine passed. The contrast between this cap and the trilby of the last image is an eloquent description of America's financially predicated/determined social system.

Between *Factory – Detroit* and the next image, *Department Store – Lincoln, Nebraska,* we have another of Frank's wonderful *caesuras.* There is no immediately apparent connection between the wall, bollards and sitting man of the last photograph and the collection of crosses on a supermarket table that is now presented. I could, again, test your credulity with ideas of industrial production in Detroit and industrial products in Nebraska, but that would be tenuous and inelegant, neither of these being characteristic of Frank's work. The most engaging connection is with the other *Americans*' image of a factory in Detroit. The first photograph, *Assembly line – Detroit* comes directly after *Crosses at scene of highway accident – U.S. 91, Idaho.* A cruciform memorial to the road-kill dead is followed by the cauldron in which the instruments of death were made. *Factory – Detroit* and *Department Store - Lincoln* mirror that progression, starting with a factory and progressing to memorial crosses. It is certainly the kind of visual play that Frank enjoys and engages in elsewhere in the book, so it is probable that this is intentional rather than fortuitous. Given the arcane nature of this connection, we can certainly see *Department Store – Lincoln, Nebraska* and the two images that follow it as a *staccato* section, a 'rat-tat-tat' of pictures, referring back to earlier photographs, ensuring that we don't forget those previous ideas and observations as we explore other aspects of Frank's vision of America. Obviously *Department Store* recapitulates the earlier section examining crosses and death. This recapitulation is another musical parallel, with so many compositions referring back to earlier motifs and movements from within 'development' and 'resolution' sections.

Department Store examines the erosion of human values by consumerism and the mass-produced. 'Hested's', as the sign in the photograph says, helps us to remember our loved ones for 69 cents. These identical white plastic cruciforms echo and reflect the cross that was held so reverently by the white-surpliced wanderer beside the *Mississippi river, Baton Rouge, Louisiana.* They recall the cross held aloft with passion, remembered in stone in *St. Francis* (actually St Junipero Serra, as we noted) and echo the quiet commemoration of the dead beneath a brilliant flare of light on the side of *U.S. 91, Idaho.* They further bring to mind the sad displacement in the face of the young mourner in *Funeral – St. Helena, South Carolina* and the weather-blasted grave in *Chinese cemetery – San Francisco.* Frank is bringing his considerations to a conclusion as we approach the end of the book. The unself-conscious manner in which these store operators degrade and commercialize this symbol is a powerful closing statement on the iconography of the cross in Frank's America.

Another prodigal and disconnected image follows, *Rodeo – New York City.* There have been other cowboy images. *Bar – Gallup, New Mexico* captured a moment of apparent tension with a solid and stalwart, hatted man four-square across the drunken composition. *Rodeo – Detroit* recorded a cigar-smoking man looking rather like the Hollywood actor Paul Newman. The current New York cowboy leans against a wire wastebasket, lighting a cigarette. He is cross-legged on a kerbstone, flanked by a puddle. He is the only obvious trace of the captioned rodeo, bizarrely transplanted into this city block. Frank has caught the heart of the dichotomy and surreality of this displaced 'cattleman', who no longer has a home on the range. The final joy of this image is the truck just along the street, behind the cowboy. In easily visible letters it advertises its manufacturer, 'Dodge'. This was the city at the heart of so many stories of the Old West, not the least of them being *Calamity Jane*, the film version of which, with Doris Day, was released in 1953. This is a gritty and unremarkable street on which a man plays out his own movie, behind his eyes.

In case we missed the point, Frank restates it for us in *Movie premiere – Hollywood.* Here, a carefully coiffured and expensively dressed *ingénue*, corsage at her bosom, fills much of the photograph despite being out of focus. This lack of clarity directs us past her, to the onlookers behind. It would appear that the young woman is a guest at the premiere and the people behind, overwhelmingly women, are spectators. Their expressions vary from smilingly engaged to the slightly perplexed look of those who adore the thing which is before them and are struggling to cope. Significantly, the lookers are not looking at our blurred subject. They look instead behind and beyond her. Like the cowboy, she too is living her own fantasy, a starlet perhaps, but not yet a star.

Lavish evening wear and carefully created hair carry on into the next image, *Charity ball – New York City.* The bejewelled lady sitting at a table accepts the embrace and kiss of the dark-haired and suited man behind. There is no suggestion here of fantasy, however: these people are dressed for and enjoying the ball mentioned in the caption. Their rich accoutrements and conspicuous consumption begin a series of four images which examine eating.

Cafeteria – San Francisco follows and contrasts bleakly with its predecessor. A pinched-faced man, hair slicked back with oil, sits alone at a table. The remains of other meals clutter the table, and the photograph's foreground. He is not shabby, but lacks the poise, care and ostentation of the couple a page back. Significantly, he also lacks company, his loneliness heightened by the obvious busyness of the place in which he eats.

A single diner is followed by a crowded room in *Drug Store – Detroit.* Here, a serried rank of mostly men sit cheek by jowl with each other, engaged with or waiting for their food and drinks. Significantly, few of them acknowledge the presence of the others. They are alone in a crowd, distanced and, in the case of the several who are looking at the camera, distrustful. Above all of this isolation hang an enormous number of signs advertising 'Orange Whip 10c', like clouds or pennants.

Coffee shop, railway station – Indianapolis finishes off the series. As with many of the images in this final section, this piece concludes Frank's discussion of the Americans eating, and of the qualities and functions of diners. A young woman behind the coffee shop's counter has turned and caught Frank taking his photograph. She has the so-often recorded expression of surprise, but she does not repeat the aggression we have observed so frequently elsewhere in the book. There is a gentleness and a kindness in her demeanour. Amidst the stainless steel, donuts and hamburgers, she has the look of a Vermeer. Her over-the-shoulder glance is powerfully reminiscent of a mirrored *Girl with a Pearl Earring* (Vermeer, c.1665, The *Mauritshuis* in *The Hague*). This is the apotheosis of the disinterested and impatient assistant in *Ranch Market – Hollywood.* Unlooked for, in a corner of a Mid-West town, there is gentleness and beauty to match anything, anywhere.

The love that inspired Vermeer, and that looks questioningly at us out of the last photograph, is the subject of the rest of the book. Typically, there are counter-images and images that punctuate: two photographs show single men and one records an unoccupied car, but the remaining ten all record some aspect of romantic or familial love. Equally typical for Frank, there are other themes invoked simultaneously. Public parks create a sub-series of six images, while the car plays a major part in the final series, with only one of the last seven images lacking a vehicular presence.

Young love occupies Frank's *Chattanooga, Tennessee.* A swarthy young man is smartly dressed with impressively padded-out shoulders. His diminutive, very fair-skinned partner is equally large of shoulder. The very white girl and the possibly Latino young man look with bemusement out of frame to the left. Their location, in Tennessee in the American South, begs many a question as to the possible source of their disapproval. In a wonderful echo within the composition, an older couple walks away from us to the image's right. The old man is fair-haired and in a light jacket, while his out-of-focus companion is dark of hair and outfit. This attractive visual symmetry is echoed by the conceptual one: youth approaches us as age walks away. New love, preparing for a life of family, house purchase and work, is in clear focus, as those who have completed these challenges become ever more distant and remote.

There is love evident too in *San Francisco.* It records a black couple, lying on the grass of a public space, high above the city.[1] They have noticed Frank and his camera and are staring confrontationally at him. The love, which is evident in their body language to each other, coexists with the dislike and the very evident threat contained in the man's expression. Love is here revealed as conditional, contextual and far from the cure-all of the so many songs soon to be penned a couple of blocks away on Haight and Ashbury.

Another park, *Belle Isle – Detroit,* is the scene for a family outing. It may be fanciful, but its figures, water and darkly silhouetted tree recall for me something of George Seurat's painting *A Sunday Afternoon on the Island of La Grand Jatte* (1884–86, Art Institute of Chicago). As with Seurat, Frank is interested in the ordinary people who occupy his space. Paris in the 1880s was in the throes of huge development and industrial expansion, so Seurat was recording the new lives of the working class and the bourgeoisie. So, too, with Frank in the American 1950s. Seurat's rich man is replaced by a serviceman in Frank's photograph, to the image's rear, and his 'lady of easy virtue' (check out the coded monkey she's holding in Seurat's painting, a symbol of base licentiousness) with a young woman holding a child on her hip and an older woman who is pregnant. The latter looks, a little sadly, out of the frame, as does the couple in the Seurat.

The sense of community generated by the assemblage in *Detroit* and the love clearly expressed by the woman and child at its centre lead into yet another park image, this time *Public park – Cleveland, Ohio.* Again, a tree is central to the image and partially protects a single man from our gaze, as he sleeps on a tatty quilt. A sense of well-being emanates from his peaceful face, and is supported by his neatly placed shoes. He is young, his hair modishly cut and he sports a tattoo on his arm. He is alone but not lonely, contentedly lying in the sun. Given the exploration of love in which we are engaged in, I wonder whether the voluptuous pin-up on his arm is important, representing his engagement with the pursuit of love, from which (perhaps because of which) he is temporarily resting? We have seen, though, that Frank repeatedly uses counter-images to interrupt a thematic flow, forcing his viewers to reconsider and re-engage with the images. I prefer to see this fashionable young man as taking time out of love, carnal or otherwise, rather than denying it.

Another tree, this time on the image's left, and another park follow. *Courthouse square – Elizabethville, North Carolina* pictures two older men sitting closely together on the roots of a large tree. Their physical proximity and their clear engagement with each other speak of another kind of love. The friends are balanced by a younger woman and a number of other men who occupy the upper third of the photograph.

Frank again moves from a group to a solitary man in a picture of yet another park with a tree at its heart. *Picnic ground – Glendale, California* pictures a random assortment of trees, benches and waste bins. The solitary man at its centre is sitting on one of these benches and views Frank, as so many others have, with suspicion. His unusually small size in relation to the image as a whole serves to emphasize further his isolation.

The quiet malaise in Glendale prefaces an explosion of life, back in *Belle Isle – Detroit.* A park is pictured again, but this time without the tree motif of the last several photographs. From now until the book closes, cars and motorbikes accompany all but one of the photographs. This movement from connection to connection has typified this final 'section', and here Frank passes the baton, as it were, recapitulating and concluding his park theme while initiating his examination of love in association with cars.

On *Belle Isle*, four small, black children occupy the rear of a cabriolet, as the adults in front focus on whatever is ahead—perhaps looking for an exit after a day of fun, or perhaps arriving and looking for somewhere to park. One boy is half-standing, with obvious pleasure and anticipation in his young face. His three fellows are sitting behind him. Their attention has been caught by something in the same direction as the camera, perhaps Frank himself, or maybe something happening nearby. They are animated, all attention and entirely at ease with each other. This is family, whether blood relatives or good friends. Significantly, one of the adults has an arm around the trilby-hatted other.

Another photograph called *Detroit* reveals an old couple sitting in their white sedan. They wear expressions of concern, perhaps uncertainty. The contrasts are clear: a young vibrant family, almost overflowing their open-top, against a roofed-over couple whose children, if they had any, have left and gone away. The balding, white-haired man and his companion are, though, still together and look out from their protected place at the bewildering and ever-changing world that has left them behind (as it now leaves behind Frank, and me also).

The third car-themed photograph in this final sequence is the slightly aberrant image I mentioned above. There is no couple or family in this photograph. It features a black saloon, which is empty, offsetting the occupied white car of the last picture. The parked car is in a just-discernible alley, dark walls rising to either side and a snippet of another vehicle just in frame at top right. Most of the high walls are visible as a sinuous reflection, drawing an arabesque of light and dark across the roof, rear window and trunk of the car. A spiderweb of girders, fire escapes or walkways is twistedly echoed at centre.

Is this, then, another of Frank's finger flicks at structure, departing from his theme in these final pages filled with romantic and filial love? Perhaps it is, but there is another possibility. The car's licence plate supports a badge saying 'Christ came to save sinners'. Above this, in the rear window, another says 'Christ died for our sins'. I've argued previously that Frank's capturing of these evangelical soundbites, which preach redemption through repentance and grace, is ironic. The relocation of the 'words of eternal life' on to a dusty automobile parked in a back alley appears to speak of the debasing influence of materialism, consumerism and advertising. Now within its sequential context, however, we might grudgingly acknowledge a less ironic possibility. Above the licence plate is the Chrysler corporate badge. This stylized cross is caught by the falling light and starkly illuminated against the almost solid black shadow in which the rest of the trunk lies. Within this shadowy and shadowed place, the lightning-like trace of brilliant sky leads vertically down the image to the cross and the badge. Christ is called the 'Man of Sorrows' and was known for his preaching to the poor and destitute, his exhortation that 'blessed are the poor in spirit', his association with lepers and prostitutes and his eventual execution at the 'Place of the Skull'. We have seen already that Frank is prepared on occasions to depict religious practice with ambivalence, even with sympathy. Given the love theme in this last sequence, might we read his depiction of Christian words here in this 'city canyon', this back alley so associated in American popular culture with mugging, drug-taking and destitution, as positive? Is it, actually, appropriate? It is an intriguing possibility, although my instinct remains with irony. In that latter case this image, while continuing with the vehicular theme, interrupts the theme of love.

Finally, as we rush towards the book's conclusion, Frank's last four images form a quadtych, following the development of a 1950s couple's love from inception to the point at which Robert and his wife Mary found themselves.

In *Public Park – Ann Arbor, Michigan*, semi-naked, bathing-suited young people are 'making out' between their cars. The cars, despite their toothy grins and chrome protrusions, seem to watch over the mating rituals like benign and protective beasts, providing escape routes from danger and shelter from prying eyes. They embody the notion of the shift of the locus of American life from the home to the car. This is their modern world and they appear as at peace with it as they could possibly be. Frank has caught one man's eye, and he looks quizzically from his front car seat out of the frame. He is questioning rather than aggressive, but eloquently reveals that the camera and the photographer are not as accepted or integrated into this world as the cars are. Frank is an outsider, the Buicks and Dodges are not. This notwithstanding, the courtship moment in modern love sits at the centre of this photograph.

City Hall – Reno, Nevada seems to me an entirely uncynical image. A young couple, barely older then the teenagers of the last image, are imaged against an opulent if rather cold interior, otherwise devoid of people. They have delight and excitement written large across their faces. The young woman is wearing a suit of Chinese silk, complete with pagodas, and the quaffed and Brylcreamed young man has on a suit. The implication is clearly that they are getting married. They are impoverished by the lack of significant others, family or friends, and they seem small and vulnerable amongst the marble and ironwork. Their vows, too, will be a legal formality in this functional building. Nonetheless, despite all of this modernity, Frank in his role as wedding photographer captures the genuine joy of the consummation of young love. This joy, full of promise and nervousness, is evidenced and underwritten by the couple's positive engagement with the camera, unusual in *The Americans*. The young woman looks shyly but happily down, while the young man smiles openly for the camera. The context, of course, is the point: people are more comfortable with a photographer at a wedding.

A more mature love is evidenced in *Indianapolis*. A couple sits on a Harley Davidson motorcycle. It is clearly a cherished object, adorned with studded leather panniers and punctuated with polished chrome. Their outfits similarly tie them to their vehicle, studded denim, a flying helmet for the woman and a Brando *Wild One*-style hat for the man. They are composed and elegant, their mirrored poses and easy physical intimacy communicating mutual reliance and sympathy. They are not, though, smiling or excited. They look a little sadly down, as if something has caught their eyes. Frank's contacts give us no clue as to what that might be: their expression is a thing of a moment as they move past him and his camera. This 'look of sadness' reveals a life that has moved on from adolescent high spirits into the more dogged and sustained challenges of adulthood. Their comfort and mutual support is, though, still very evident.

Finally, then, to *U.S. 90, en route to Del Rio, Texas*. We have looked at this image in depth already. I've described it, along with *Barbershop McLellanville* as Frank's signature, his revelation of himself to us, his declaration of authorship. Seeing this image in its sequential context reinforces this. Having examined courtship, the nervous excitement of commitment and the quality of companionship that accompanies years spent in a relationship, Frank here figures his own place. He has examined the love of older people in many earlier images: the couple in their white car in *Detroit*, the pair blurrily receding in *Chattanooga, Tennessee*, the couple at the *Charity ball – New York City* or in the *Hotel Lobby – Miami Beach*, but these are conjectural, based on imagination and observation rather than experience. It is fitting that the book's final image, the last picture of twelve mostly concerned with human relationships, and the final photograph of the quadtych examining modern love, should be intensely personal. There is no conjecture or imagination here: this is Frank's reality. The tired face of the woman in the car is the face of his wife, sharing both his physical journey and his metaphorical journey, intimately connected and concerned with the project which her photographic portrait concludes. Frank's own blood flows in the sleeping child leaning against his mother. This photograph, finally, stands with the million kitsch, trite, clichéd and banal images taken by lovers and parents of their loved ones and children. This is

Frank's world, individual and particular, but also participating, through the implication of continuity in the final four images, in the same world as all the others who share his time and his space.

Note

1. I found this park; it's in Alamo Square, San Francisco. The Victorian board houses, locally called the Painted Ladies, are still as they were in Frank's photograph.

Conclusion

The Americans is essentially a work of prophecy. Frank set out to make an 'observation and record of what one naturalized American finds to see in the United States' (Frank 1954, in Greenough 2009: 362).[1] He calls it an 'observation', but it was not designed as 'documentary': he also said in his Guggenheim Fellowship application 'it is only partly documentary in nature: one of its aims is more artistic than the word documentary implies' (Frank 1954, in Greenough 2009: 362). Frank was concerned with expressing his own opinions. He told his parents, 'I am working very hard… to give an opinion in my photos of America' (Frank 1955, in Tucker and Brookman 1986: 28). He was happy to criticize: 'Opinion often consists of a kind of criticism. But criticism can come out of love' (Frank, in Maloney 1958: 115). Opinion and criticism belong more to notions of art than reportage. Frank could not find a name for the synthesis he intended to attempt, but it clearly existed somewhere between art and document.

The relationship between Walker Evans' *American Photographs* and *The Americans* has been noted. Frank believed that Evans' photography could 'transform destiny into awareness' (Frank, in Maloney 1958: 115), that he could depict in visual terms those previously undefined forces which are at work in the world around him. His photographs brought these hidden forces into the light. Frank wanted the same for his work: 'I speak of the things that are there, anywhere and everywhere—easily found, not easily interpreted' (Frank 1954, in Greenough 2009: 362). This is the role and language of the prophet.

Biblical prophecy was not foretelling the future, but the public declaration of truth. The prophet Samuel confronted King David after the king's seduction of Bathsheba and the murder of her husband. He presented David's actions to him in a metaphor, and sought his judgement. David condemned the perpetrator to death, thus condemning himself. His own judgement struck far deeper than that of another, and he was humbled by his knowledge of the truth. Samuel led the King of Israel to this place not by polemical speeches or rallies but by revealing in a story the true nature of David's actions (Anon. n.d.: 12:1). In the same way, Frank's refusal to take any easy options expresses his powerful and precise vision.

The Americans is radically structured. It reflects the sequence of moments that together constructed Frank's experience. It refuses the constraints of linear logic or the directed reading of an accompanying text. It works intuitively, eschewing a linguistic or rational understanding, like the novels of Joyce or Kerouac, the poetry of Ginsberg, the jazz of Kenton, Parker and Coltrane and the paintings of Pollock and de Kooning. Frank was reacting against his conviction that 'photography today is accepted without question and is presumed to be understood by all' (Frank, in Maloney 1958: 115). His work requires extended engagement and, as with Samuel and David, the denouement, when it comes, is therefore far more powerful.

Frank looked, sensibly, into the American flag for a glimpse of the faces behind, beneath and within it. He found uncertain people, nervously watching their nation's celebrations with a defensive hand before their mouths. There were also people who were relaxed and confident around the flag, casual and comfortable in its presence. He saw it signify the history of its nation as it rubbed cheeks with the kitsch and tawdry and cosied up with the industrial and mass-produced. He saw that, for some, identity lost within the flag was an act of obeisance, the individuals thus stripped being complicit and willing. Frank found the reality of the American Dream hiding behind its most obvious symbol. His assessment is simultaneously pointed, critical and comic.

The car and the road revealed, beneath their tawdry concrete and paint, the needs of a nation's dreams. Frank described these dreamers hurtling toward their destiny, procreating between cars, protected by cars, killed by cars and worshipping these manifestations of the American need to journey. The hope of a better world, a new life, all of humanity's dreams and desires are symbolized in the New World by chrome, rubber and steel. His assessment was equivocal. In his subversion of the advertisements of Standard Oil, Frank both criticized and embraced the American fixation with roads.

A new civilization needs a new faith. Frank identified a pantheon of icons and laid them before his audience for homage. Again, he equivocates. Petrol pumps are wondered at, not rubbished, jukeboxes sound the words of a hundred new creeds, lour over babies and are a new hope in the darkness of an unemployed Vegas day or a candy store night in New York City.

Frank expounded the truth of the America he saw against an establishment capable of *The Family of Man*. Evans called it 'mindless pictorial sales talk around fashionable, guilty and therefore bogus heartfeeling' (Evans, in Maloney 1958: 90). This was the pictorial manifestation of America's understanding of itself and its world. Frank sought to challenge it: 'America is an interesting country, but there is a lot here that I do not like and that I would never accept. I am also trying to show this in my photos' (Frank in Tucker and Brookman 1986: 28).

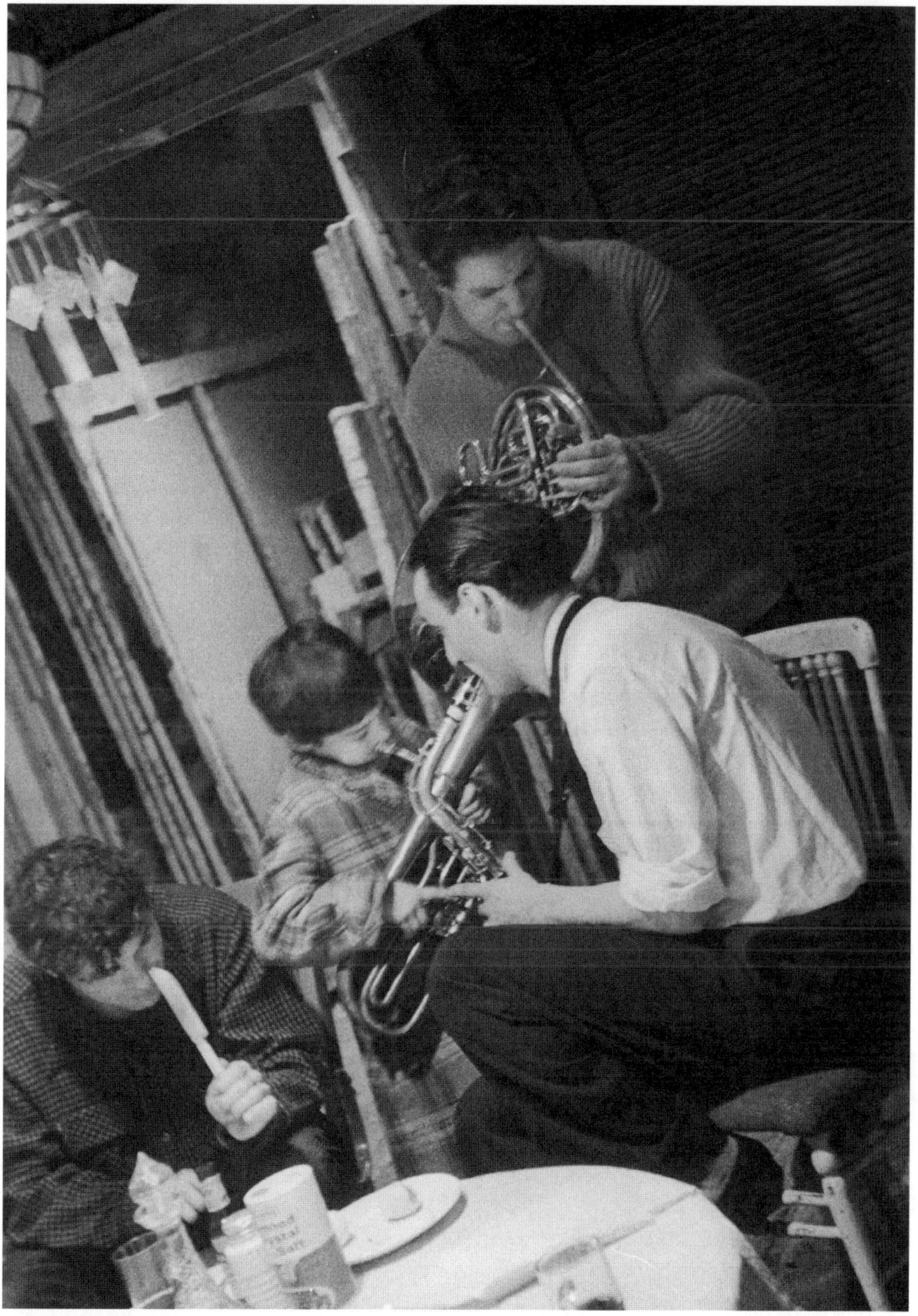

On the set of the Robert Frank film *Pull My Daisy*. Poet Gregory Corso, Pablo Frank on euphonium, painter Larry Rivers on saxophone, and musician David Amram on Fench horn, 1 Jan 1959. (Photo by John Cohen/Getty Images)

Finally, Frank concludes his examination with a clear and very personal visual statement. He describes his purpose. This is a book about America seen through his eyes, conditioned and influenced as he is by those who went before, but nonetheless with something personal to say. His careful consideration of this new place uncovered claims that could not be substantiated and hopes that must lie unfulfilled. The direction and desires of these people, characterized by a flaming neon arrow, must surely take them somewhere, but this place is yet to be and Frank cannot see it, much less go there. He finally remains ambivalent, in the here-and-now of a dusty roadside, with a shrug.

Frank revealed America to itself, not through propaganda or convoluted argument, but by presenting one man's vision. He brought it, half-whispered and guessed at, into the material existence of tone on photographic paper. Like the prophets, he expounded things at the edge of vision, things half-noticed or ignored. This man, along with many others, absorbed the images of a new civilization. He actualized it visually in a book of photographs. This is the artist as prophet, shaman and conscience. The vision, though unquestionably personal, was more resonant than he could ever have imagined: 'I knew that I had something, but I didn't even know I had America.' (Frank, in Wheeler 1977: 22)

Note

1. The full sentence reads, '... observation and record of what one naturalised American finds to see in the United States that signifies the kind of civilization born here and spreading elsewhere.' (Frank, in Greenough 2009: 362)

References

Agee, J., and Evans, W. (1941), *Let Us Now Praise Famous Men*, Boston: Houghton Mifflin.

Alexander, S. (1997), 'Robert Frank Discusses the Americans at George Eastman House, 17 and 18 August 1967', *Katalog: Journal of Photography and Video*, 9(4), Odense: Museet for Fotokunst.

The Americans website (2010), http://www.steidlville.com/books/695-The-Americans.html, accessed 20 January.

Anonymous (1958), 'The Second Book of Samuel', *The Bible*, London: Collins.

Apollinaire, G. (1949), *The Cubist Painters: Aesthetic Meditations 1913*, New York: Wittenborn Schulz.

Aristotle (2003), *Poetics*, London: Penguin.

Avedon, R., Brodovitch, A. and Capote, T. (1959), *Observations*, New York: Simon and Schuster.

Benedek, L. (1954), *The Wild One*, UCA, 1954.

Brandt, B. (1936), *The English at Home*, London: Batsford.

—— (1948), *A Camera in London*, London: Focal Press.

Brodovitch, A. (1945), *Ballet*, New York: Augustin.

Brookman, A. and Brookman P. (1986), *Fire in the East: A Portrait of Robert Frank* (video documentary), Houston: Houston Museum of Fine Arts/Houston Public Television (KUHT).

Bunnell Peter (1977), 'Remembering Limelight', in *Helen Gee and the Limelight: A Pioneering Photography Gallery of the Fifties*, New York: Carlton Gallery.

Butler, D. (1953), *Calamity Jane*, Warner Brothers.

Caldwell, E. and Bourke-White, M. (1937), *You Have Seen Their Faces*, New York: Modern Age Books.

Camus, A. (2005 [1942]), *The Myth of Sisyphus*, London: Penguin.

Capa, R. and Gerda T. (1938), *Death in the Making*, New York: Covici-Friede.

Cartier-Bresson, H. (1952), *Images à la Sauvette* (The Decisive Moment), Paris: Éditions Verve.

Cassady, C. (2007), *Off the Road: Twenty Years with Cassady, Kerouac and Ginsberg*, London: Black Spring Press.

Charters, A. (2007), 'Introduction', in J. Kerouac, *On the Road*, London: Penguin.

Clay, J. (1978), *Modern Art*, Secaucus, NJ: Chartwell Books.

Coke, Van Deren and Du Pont, D. (1986), *Photography, A Facet of Modernism*, New York: Hudson Hills Press/San Francisco: Museum of Modern Art.

Corbett, John (1995), 'Ephemera Underscored: Writing Around Free Improvisation', in Krin Gabbard (ed.), *Jazz Among the Discourses*, Durham, NC: Duke University Press.

Cuirara, C. (2002), *Beat Poets*, London: Everyman.

Day, J. (2008), *The Politics of Navigation: Globalisation, Music and Composition*, Saarbrucken: Verlag Dr Muller.

de Beauvoir, S. (1953), *America Day by Day*, New York: Grove Press.

de Saussure, F. (1995), *Course in General Linguistics,* London: Gerald Duckworth and Co. Ltd.

Eliot, T.S. (1932), *Selected Essays 1917–1932,* London: Faber and Faber.

Evans, W. (1995 [1938]), *American Photographs*, New York: Museum of Modern Art.

—— (1957), 'Robert Frank', *US Camera Annual 1958*, New York: US Camera Publishing Corp.

Fitch, S. (1976), *Diesels and Dinosaurs, Photos from the US Highway*, Berkeley, CA: Long Run Press.

Fitzgerald, F. Scott (1994 [1926]), *The Great Gatsby*, London: Penguin.

Ford, J. (1940), *The Grapes of Wrath,* 20th Century Fox.

Frank, R. (1957), 'A Statement', *US Camera Annual 1958*, New York: US Camera Publishing Corp.

—— (1958), *Les Americaines*, Paris: Robert Delpire.

—— (1959), *The Americans*, New York: Grove Press.

—— (1961), 'Black and White are the Colors of Photography', *Aperture*, 9(1), New York: Aperture Foundation.

—— (1968), *The Americans*, New York: Aperture/Museum of Modern Art.

—— (1989), *The Lines of My Hand*, New York: Pantheon.

—— (1991), *Robert Frank*, London: Thames and Hudson/Paris: Centre National de la Photographie.

—— (1993), *The Americans*, Zurich: Scalo.

—— (1994), *Black, White and Things* (facsimile of 1952 edition), Zurich: Scalo.

—— (2008), *The Americans*, Gottingen: Steidl/Washington: National Gallery of Art.

Frank, R., Bischof, W. and Verger, P. (1956), *Indiens pas Morts*, Paris: Robert Delpire.

Ginsberg, A. (1956), *Howl*, San Francisco: City Lights Books.

Greenough, S. (2009), *Looking In*, Washington: National Gallery of Art/Steidl.

Guthrie, W. (1997 [1945]), 'This Land is Your Land', *Woody Guthrie: This Land is Your Land: The Asch Recordings Volume 1*, Washington: Smithsonian Folkways.

Hardy, T. (1917), *Moments of Vision and Other Miscellaneous Verses*, London: Dodo Press.

Hicks, W. (1952), *Words and Pictures*, New York: Harper Brothers.

Hitchcock, A. (1960), *Psycho*, Shamley Productions/Paramount/Universal.

Hunter, J. (1987), *Image and Word*, Cambridge, MA: Harvard University Press.

Ilf, I. and Petrov, E. (1937), *Little Golden America: Two Famous Soviet Humourists Survey These United States*, New York: Farrar and Rinehart.

Janis, E. Paris and MacNeil, W. (1977), *Photography Within the Humanities*, Danbury, NH: Addison House.

Johnson, W. (ed.) (1989), *The Pictures are a Necessity: Robert Frank in Rochester, NY November 1988*, New York: Rochester Film and Photo Consortium and International Museum of Photography.

Joyce, J. (1993), *Ulysses*, London: Penguin.

Kazan, E. (1951), *A Streetcar Named Desire*, Warner Brothers.

Keller, U. (1986), *The Highway as Habitat, A Roy Stryker Documentation, 1943–1955*, Santa Barbara, CA: University of California.

Kerouac, J. (1972), *On the Road*, London: Penguin.

—— (1992), 'The Essentials of Spontaneous Prose', in A. Charters (ed.), *The Portable Beat Reader*, New York: Viking Penguin.

Klein, W. (1996 [1956]), *Life is Good and Good for You in New York,* New York: Dewi Lewis.

Koeppen, W. (1959), *American Journey*, Frankfurt: Suhrkamp.

Lacan, J. (1968), *The Language of the Self: The Function of Language in Psychoanalysis,* Baltimore, MD: Johns Hopkins University Press.

Libsohn, S. (1945), 'Trucking Story', *The Lamp*, Standard Oil of New Jersey.

Livingston, J. (1992), *The New York School Photographs 1936–1963*, New York: Stewart, Tabori and Chang.

Maloney, T. (1958), *U. S. Camera Annual,* New York, U. S. Camera Publishing Corp.

Manchester, W. (1989), *In Our Time*, London: South Bank Centre.

Marx, K. (1977), *Critique of Hegel's Philosophy of Right,* Cambridge: Cambridge University Press.

Mayr, O. and Post, R. (1981), *Yankee Enterprise: The Rise of The American System of Manufactures,* Washington, DC: Smithsonian Books.

McBride, J. (1989), *Great Balls of Fire*, Metro Goldwyn Mayer.

Merz, C. (1928), *The Great American Bandwagon*, New York: The John Day Company.

Milestone, L. (1939), *Of Mice and Men,* Hal Roach Studios.

Mingus, S. (1997), 'Mingus', *Goblin Web Magazine*, 8, http://www.sonic.net/~goblin/8mingus.html, accessed 20 May.

Owen, W. (1994), *The Poems Of Wilfred Owen,* Ware: Wordsworth.

Papageorge, Tod (1981), *Walker Evans and Robert Frank: An Essay on Influence*, New Haven, CN: Yale University Art Gallery.

Plattner, S. W. (1983), *Roy Stryker: USA, 1943 – 1950. The Standard Oil (New Jersey) Photography Project,* Houston, University of Texas Press.

Ray, N. (1955), *Rebel Without a Cause,* Warner Brothers.

Riis, J. (1998), *How the Other Half Live: Studies Among the Tenements of New York*, London: Penguin.

Schuh, G. (1957), 'Robert Frank', *Camera*, August, New York: US Camera Publishing Corp.

Shakespeare, W. (2007), *Othello*, London: Penguin.

Steichen, E. (1955), *The Family of Man*, New York: Museum of Modern Art.

Stryker, R. (1946), transcript of lectures at the Design Institute, Chicago, August, held in the Roy Stryker Papers, Photographic Archives, Ekstrom Library, University of Louisville. Also available in U. Keller (1986), *The Highway as Habitat, A Roy Stryker Documentation, 1943–1955*, Santa Barbara, CA: University of California, 201–2.

Tucker, A. and Brookman, P. (1986), *New York to Nova Scotia*, New York: Graphic Society Books/Houston: Museum of Fine Arts.

Tudor-Hart, M. (1986), *Das Auge Des Gewissens*, Berlin: Foto-Taschenbuch.

Various (1958), 'First Letter to the Corinthians', *The Bible*, London: Collins.

Various, 'An Off-Beat View of the U.S.A.', *Popular Photography*, 46(5), n.p.

Various (2009), *Writings from the Zen Masters*, London: Penguin.

Wall, A. (2009), *COOL*, London: BBC.

Wheeler, D. (1977), 'Robert Frank Interviewed', *Criteria*, 3(2), n.p.

Wilcox, F. (1956), *Forbidden Planet*, MGM.

Photographs in *The Americans*

Index